Read It Again...
of John's Creek
3630 Peachtree Pkwy.
Suwanee, GA 30024

The Ad Game

The Ad Game
Playing to Win

G. ROBERT COX

EDWARD J. McGEE

Prentice Hall
Englewood Cliffs, New Jersey 07632

Library of Congress Cataloging-in-Publication Data

Cox, G. Robert.
  The ad game: playing to win/G. Robert Cox, Edward J. McGee.
  p. cm.
  Includes index.
  ISBN 0-13-004490-3
  1. Advertising—Handbooks, manuals, etc.   2. Sales promotion—
Handbooks, manuals, etc.   I. McGee, Edward J.   II. Title.
HF5823.C64   1990
659.1—dc19   89-3478
                                                     CIP

Cover design: Lundgren Graphics, Ltd.
Manufacturing buyer: Mary Ann Gloriande

 ©1990 by Prentice-Hall, Inc.
A Division of Simon & Schuster
Englewood Cliffs, New Jersey 07632

All rights reserved. No part of this book may be
reproduced, in any form or by any means,
without permission in writing from the publisher.

The publisher offers discounts on this book when ordered
in bulk quantities. For more information, write:

> Special Sales/College Marketing
> Prentice Hall
> College Technical and Reference Division
> Englewood Cliffs, NJ 07632

Printed in the United States of America

10 9 8 7 6 5 4 3 2 1

ISBN   0-13-004490-3

PRENTICE-HALL INTERNATIONAL (UK) LIMITED, *London*
PRENTICE-HALL OF AUSTRALIA PTY, LIMITED, *Sydney*
PRENTICE-HALL CANADA INC., *Toronto*
PRENTICE-HALL HISPANOAMERICANA, S.A., *Mexico*
PRENTICE-HALL OF INDIA PRIVATE LIMITED, *New Delhi*
PRENTICE-HALL OF JAPAN, INC., *Tokyo*
SIMON & SCHUSTER ASIA PTE. LTD., *Singapore*
EDITORA PRENTICE-HALL DO BRASIL, LTDA., *Rio de Janeiro*

Contents

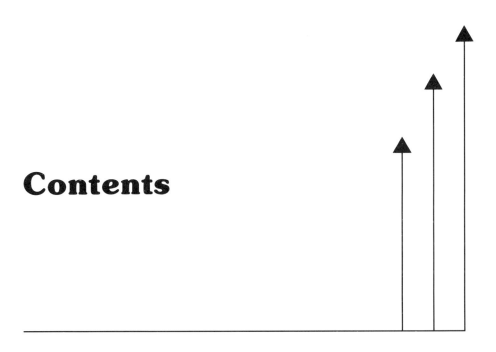

3 PRINTING AND PRODUCTION   38

*Knowing how to control production costs—a vital
communications management asset.*

4 SALES PROMOTION, PRODUCT LITERATURE, AND PRESENTATION MATERIALS   54

*The forgotten media: Almost all that your customers
or prospects will ever know about your company they
will find out from the materials you provide.*

5 PUBLICITY   78

The best things in life are free. Publicity, although not altogether "free," is usually one of the least costly and most effective promotional tools you can use.

6 DIRECT MAIL   95

The "Rifle-Shot" approach—hitting known targets where they live.

7 SPACE ADVERTISING   113

The "Buckshot" approach—hitting various targets over a wide range of prospects.

8 ELECTRONIC MEDIA: RADIO, TELEVISION, TELEMARKETING, AND OUTDOOR ADVERTISING   140

Further illustration of the "Buckshot" approach.

9 TRADE SHOWS   161

Your prospects call on you—be prepared to "Show and Tell."

10 THE CREATIVE EFFORT   183

*Copy, visualization, layout—the big payoff goes
to the creative manager.*

11 PARTING SHOTS   198

*Experience is still the best teacher. Nothing new under
the sun, but variations keep us going strong. Memories that
bless and burn.*

INDEX   219

Preface

This book has been written to bring aid and comfort to that most fortunate adventurer who has just entered the wonderful world of marketing communications in a small- to medium-sized company.

The reason we say such an individual is most fortunate is expressed best by Franklin Delano Roosevelt: "If I were starting life over, I am inclined to think I would go into the advertising business in preference to almost any other. The general raising of the standards of modern civilization among all groups of people during the past half century would have been impossible without the spreading of the knowledge of higher standards by means of advertising."

Whether your company markets industrial goods, consumer goods, or services, we feel certain that the following pages will provide you with literally scores of ideas to make you a more effective, productive, creative, and profitable communicator.

One quick point should be made about that word *communications*. Even though this book is directed toward advertising, sales promotion, and publicity, you, as the newly minted head of the ad department or at the publicity desk or wherever, will find yourself in the communications business. And, as a communicator, you will be drawn into all kinds of fascinating areas—everything from editing sales letters and directing corporate press conferences to developing creative ad campaigns will be in your domain.

Depending on the size of the company and the type of product lines, the administrator of a company's communications operation can carry any one of a horde of different titles. Typical labels are: Advertising Manager, Product Manager, Marketing Communications Director, Promotion Manager, Marketing Coordinator, and Assistant Sales Manager. And in some firms, either small in size or highly technical in product line, the promotional effort is directed and implemented by such lofty officials as the President or the CEO. Whatever the title, the goal of this book is to offer the person in charge of communications specific, usable information drawn from years of actual work experiences.

We have tried to concentrate on fundamental and proven ways to promote sales for technical, industrial, and consumer product lines, and have resisted temptations to write textbook copy on marketing theory or business philosophy and the like. Our goal is to present you with material that is well defined, practical, and—most important—*usable.*

This is not to say that we have neglected to show many instances where basic marketing principles have been used to direct promotional campaigns, nor have we avoided getting into creative direction and approaches employed to achieve specific promotional goals.

We have attempted to show that there is very little magic in producing successful sales promotion and advertising campaigns and that this success relies more on the consistent application of basic techniques rather than on tricky headlines, gimmicky art, and one-shot promotional splashes.

We believe that, while a small- or medium-sized company can do without a titled promotional manager, it cannot do without the functions such an individual must perform on a regular basis.

Successful sales promotion depends on the manager who can develop a well-coordinated plan and implement it just as any other important management operation must be implemented—regularly—not on a hit-or-miss basis.

The Ad Game: Playing to Win will show you how to draw up an effective promotional plan and illustrate specifically how your plan should then be executed. The text also includes many practical forms and checklists that you can adapt to your day-to-day working needs.

Our attempt has been to keep this work as simple as possible and to illustrate how, step by step, professional campaigns are put together. We want to show the recently placed "communicator" how, by following certain ground rules, he or she can produce the same kind of successful, effective promotions as the "pros."

This book is designed to be used as a "how to" reference and to assist the executive who handles promotion with ideas and methods on producing the most cost-effective advertising and sales promotional programs. As that executive, we wish you the best of luck in the most exciting and rewarding of careers.

Communications: The Basics

1

The primary objective of advertising and sales promotion is to present a selling message in such a compelling way that it will persuade a prospect to find out more about and eventually buy the items being promoted. In ninety-nine out of one hundred instances, the most effective way involves simplicity and clarity. After all, our goal is not to confound. As self-evident as this may seem, it is often forgotten by those who believe they must flaunt their engineering degrees and communicate only technical jargon, or by those English majors who, in trying to write erudite consumer promotions, wind up selling only confusion.

INDUSTRIAL ADVERTISING

In order to produce optimum results, industrial advertising must communicate facts. The more clearly, simply, and directly it does so, the more productive it will be. Usually industrial advertising features more objectivity than consumer goods advertising. The latter can use broader, more subjective, and, often, strictly emotional appeals.

Many people feel that an industrial ad manager must be more disciplined and precise than his or her counterpart in the consumer field—that he or she must build sales stories on factual rather than emotional foundations.

This is not to say that industrial advertising approaches need be dull or ignore high-impact creative approaches. On the contrary, the brutal competition for a buyer's attention challenges all of an industrial communicator's ingenuity. That challenge becomes all the greater since he or she must work within the confines of reality, logic, and common sense.

CONSUMER ADVERTISING

In many instances the individual responsible for the promotional material behind consumer goods or services seems to have greater latitude than his or her industrial counterpart. Consumer advertising can take two alternate routes, factual and emotional, and remain effective in either one. However, consumer advertising does usually have more leeway in reaching the basic emotions than do industrial promotions. The consumer goods spokesperson can talk about status symbols or welfare of loved ones or achievement or self-esteem much more readily and credibly than the industrial goods communications manager.

THE OBJECT OF THE GAME IS TO SELL

All advertising—consumer, industrial, technical, or whatever—is "selling" in the sense that you use promotions to seek out, contact, and influence new prospects, arouse interest in your target market, and create a preference for your products or services over those of your competitors. To plunge into the advertising world you need not be a creative genius nor possess vast insights into human behavior. Instead, you must simply understand some basic rules and apply them with an abundance of straightforward logical thinking. You must also explore the various promotional avenues that are open to you and have a rough idea of what they cost. Volumes have been written on "How to Communicate" and even more specifically how to create effective advertising. Both the newcomer and the seasoned pro are well advised to read some of these books, especially those dealing with advertising and sales promotion. You should also subscribe to advertising trade publications such as *Business Marketing* and *Advertising Age,* which are directed to both industrial and consumer areas. It is also recommended that you subscribe to some of the many publications on marketing, sales promotion, and advertising that are now available.

ADVERTISING COPY

Because copywriting is the bedrock of most promotional efforts, we must recognize its importance at the outset. We urge you to study books that cover basic writing skills, such as *The New Guide to Better Writing* by Rudolf Flesch and A. H. Lass, *Elements of Style* by William Strunk, Jr., and E. B. White, and other works that emphasize clear, concise writing and help you to become more comfortable and effective with the written word. Writing skills will be your primary tool and your paramount asset in this world of communications. Again, this may seem obvious to most people, but many individuals, students in particular, think they can somehow become professional communicators without learning how to write. Those who believe this only fool and hurt themselves.

A case in point: The authors remember giving a course to a class of students at a leading drama school who were hopeful of becoming radio announcers. We were appalled by the number of students who rejected any course material in basic writing skills. It was a painful process to make these fledgling announcers understand that, even though their work in radio would be verbal, they would be obliged to prepare written material ahead of air time if they were to come across at all well. "We're not here to become writers," they complained. They sincerely believed that once they were behind a microphone the wit, charm, and patter would roll off the tip of their tongue without any difficulty. Nice dream, but it does not usually work that way. Success comes to those who prepare for it. So, like the Boy Scouts say, "Be prepared."

The way you learn to write is to write, write, write. We had to convince these students that something had to be put in before anything clever rolled out and that written preparation of material was necessary for any kind of success. In order to make the point we brought in some of Boston's foremost announcers who informed the students that for every hour on the air at least four hours of writing time was required. Writing is essential, even in "verbal" communications.

MARKETING RESEARCH

Important as writing (copy) is, it is not the only basic with which communicators should concern themselves. At the very outset of developing a communications program, attention should be given to some research in the marketing arena. The specific type of research undertaken will depend on the company and the product or service offered for sale.

As an example, the authors developed a series of annual marketing research studies for one of their clients. The client, an insurance agency, competed with a host of other agents in his market area. He undertook newspaper, radio, and outdoor advertising to develop sales and we convinced him that periodic field surveys could enhance the effectiveness of his promotion.

We have used the procedure we initially developed for this client (with variations, of course) to help other clients. First, we designed a brief questionnaire. The topics covered included asking respondents (1) from whom they currently purchased home or casualty insurance; (2) why they patronized that agent; (3) what would motivate them to drop one agent and pick up another; and (4) if they remembered any of our client's advertising and in what medium they had seen or heard it.

The results of the surveys enabled us each year to put together more and more persuasive advertising based on the data we collected. Further, we had a consistent evaluation of the medium that should receive the lion's share of our promotional budget. The bottom line, as you well know, is the payoff in profits. For this client, the payoff was excellent. In each of five successive years that we conducted the survey and followed its directions, the number of auto and home insurance policies sold increased from 10 to 18 percent.

IMPLEMENTING YOUR RESEARCH PROGRAM

How do you implement a research project such as this to help yourself? You could contact a professional marketing research firm to prepare a questionnaire for you, handle the interviewing, and evaluate the results. If you follow this course, expect to pay a hefty fee.

Or you might do as we did. After developing a questionnaire that touches all the bases you want to touch, we suggest you contact a marketing professor at a nearby two-year or four-year college. Explain that you would like to have him or her provide you with the names of a couple of students who are outgoing, personable, and comfortable when talking with strangers. In our case, we made use of two students each year. We then supplied these students with a couple hundred copies of the questionnaire and instructed them to conduct shopping mall intercept interviews.

In each of four shopping centers we asked students to interview fifty individuals. The students wore prominent lapel badges showing their names, their college name, and the fact that they were conducting a market survey. If you follow this proven procedure, you will find that your students will receive courteous responses from four out of every five persons they approach. Do not expect these students to handle this assignment on a no-charge basis. We paid their auto expenses and a reasonably low, but acceptable, hourly wage.

The following is a highly successful questionnaire that helped the client develop effective and productive promotional programs.

◀──

Sample: C&B Image Study Questionnaire

"How do you do? My name is _____ . I am a Marketing student at _____ College, working on a market research study. I'd appreciate just a couple of minutes of your time to ask you a few questions. May I? Thank you."

1. Have you ever heard of Caddell & Byers Insurance Agency?
   Yes _____   No _____
   What is your opinion of this company to do business with?

Most desirable _____   So-so _____   Undesirable _____
Don't Know _____

2. Have you ever seen any advertising for Caddell & Byers?
   Yes _____   No _____
   Where did you see the advertising for C&B? _____
   (If newspaper is mentioned, try to get name of paper.)

3. (If answer to #2 is "Yes.") What can you remember about the advertising?
   _____

4. Which is most important to you when buying insurance (automobile and/or homeowner's)?
   Price _____   Service _____

5. How important is it that you know the name and that you are familiar with the face of the particular individual with whom you do business in your agent's office?
   Very important _____   Somewhat important _____
   No importance _____

   Would you please tell me what town you live in? _____
   Observations and comments _____
   Location of interview _____   M _____   F _____
   Under 25 _____   25-50 _____   Over 50 _____
   Student's name: _____   Date: _____

   ──▶

Perhaps your research activities might be closer to some of the other examples you will find in later chapters. The point is, some research might be important in helping you determine to whom you want to talk, what you want to say to them, and what media you want to use to reach them.

The above example comes from the consumer promotion field. Research can be just as vital in the case of industrial advertising. For instance, the authors developed a study to determine prime prospects and the most effective media to reach them for a manufacturer of antistatic carpeting designed for companies with computer facilities.

This involved a survey of national distributors, dealers, and possible users of the carpeting to find out which of the trade and industrial magazines they read and recommended. Rather than being conducted in person on a face-to-face basis, this survey was carried out on the telephone and through the use of mail questionnaires. Regardless of your approach, research might be one of the basics you do not want to overlook.

OTHER FUNDAMENTAL AREAS

So far in this chapter we have introduced the importance of copywriting and marketing research. The writing of copy will be covered in more depth in Chapter 10, The Creative Effort. Additional areas that will be covered in detail in upcoming chapters involve proper media selection and the pros and cons of each medium; visualizing and layout; mechanical production; the use of promotional specialties; and, underlying all these, ways in which creativity can be developed to bring out the very best in each.

FOLLOWING UP THE INQUIRIES
(MINING THE GOLD)

No discussion of communications basics would be complete without an explanation of inquiry follow-up systems and how they work. After all, communications is a two-way street and if you are not getting messages back from the marketplace (positive or negative—but hopefully more positive), then you had better take a hard look at the messages you are sending out.

The most traceable results you can produce for all the time and money spent on your promotional program are the inquiries it produces. Therefore, it is in your best interest, as well as your company's, to make sure that you keep tight control over inquiries and that you are responding to them as quickly as possible. It is equally critical that you inform the salespeople that someone out there has inquired, that you have sent appropriate materials, and that the ball is now in the sales department's court.

Sometimes the sales department takes charge of the original inquiry and follows up from the start. We have found, however, that when the communication operation (advertising function) is set up to respond as soon as an inquiry is received, things move a lot faster all the way down the line.

TYPICAL INQUIRY FOLLOW-UP OPERATION

First, the prospect *must be contacted immediately* (within one week) with the following:

1. A "thank you" cover letter responding to the inquiry.
2. A package of promotional materials, which hopefully conforms to the information the prospect has requested.
3. The name, address, and phone number of the local sales contact.
4. A postpaid reply card offering more specific help.

Sample: Initial Inquiry Response Letter

(Personalized to inquiring prospect)

Good Morning!

Thank you for your inquiry.

We are enclosing a brochure covering some of the styles and colors available in our COMPU-CARPET/COMPU-TILE lines of Computer-Grade static-dissipating carpeting.

Hopefully, the enclosed brochure will be of help and we will have our representative contact you shortly to provide whatever assistance you may need.

In the meantime, if you provide more specific information about your particular application on the enclosed reply card, we will get back to you immediately.

Our sales representative in your area is:
Name: _____
Address: _____
Phone: _____

Sincerely,

―――――――――――――――――――――――――――――▶

At the same time the above response letter is sent to the prospect, the following should be sent to the salespeople in the area where the inquiry originated.

◀―――――――――――――――――――――――――――――

Sample: Informing Sales Representative of Inquiry

Dear (Rep personalized):

We have received the following inquiry(ies) from a prospect in your area. Please take the action you feel is most appropriate, fill in the inquiry follow-up form, and return within two weeks.

Sincerely,

―――――――――――――――――――――――――――――▶

The above letter is sent to company territorial salespeople or representatives along with the following three-part form. The original of the form is kept in the advertising department. The first copy is sent to the sales manager and the second copy to the in-field salesperson for completion and return to the originating advertising department. Following this procedure will provide important data on sales, advertising effectiveness, and media selection. The entire system is easily auto-mated on a computer program such as "PFS First Choice" which has Merge and Reporting capabilities.

Sample: Inquiry Follow-Up Form (See Fig. 1–1)

(Inquirer information filled in at home office)

(Information from advertising department)

       Prospect's name _____

       Company _____

       Address _____

       Telephone _____ Date of inquiry _____

       Source of inquiry: Mag _____ D/M _____

       Publicity _____ Phone _____

       Other _____

       Date to sales manager _____ Date to rep _____

(Information to be returned from sales department)

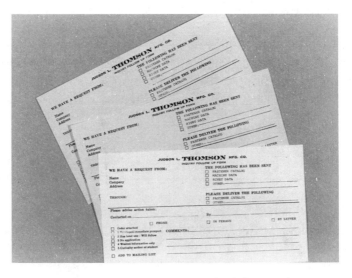

Figure 1–1. Typical three-part inquiry follow-up form.

Sales follow-up information call made (date) _____
Type of call: Phone _____ Letter _____ In person _____
Post-call determination _____
No immediate need—Will call again _____
No real interest (literature collector) _____
Asked for quote _____
Made sale _____
Comments _____
_____

Salesperson: _____ Report Date: _____

All of the above inquiry-handling information can be tailored to suit your particular situation and requirements, and the general procedures indicated can be easily computerized for quick, sure control.

THE CALL REPORT
(KEEPING THE RECORD STRAIGHT)

One last communication "basic" is what the ad agencies refer to as the "Call Report." Among other things, it is used as a basis for an agency to bill clients for time spent and work performed. You can use this device to keep track of your activities and advise your management of your accomplishments. It also covers you in the event you need verification of agreements and OKs.

The following is a typical Call Report covering three divisions of a company over a one-week period. It simply restates what occurred during various management meetings. The following report turned out to be particularly important because a sales manager forgot that he had committed an ad to a magazine, and, since it was in the Call Report, we did not have to argue about money being spent without authorization.

The specifics here are not important but the format may be useful in keeping your thinking concise and clear.

Sample: Call Report

CALL REPORT COVERING MEETINGS
HELD WEEK OF (DATE)
COMPANY NAME:
DEPARTMENT: Software, Calibration, and Cassette
FROM:
TO:

Meeting #1   Software Division   (day) (date)
                  For Client: Madeline M. and Joseph F.
                  For Agency: Bob C., Ed M., and Lynn S.
Meeting #2   Calibration Division   (day) (date)
                  For Client: John F.
                  For Agency: Bob C., Barbara K., and Lynn S.
Meeting #3   Cassette Division   (day) (date)
                  For Client: Jack D.
                  For Agency: Bob C.

The following covers the high points of our meetings with all divisions
in Natick during the week of (date).

Meeting #1: Software Division

   All materials required for the Comdex Show in Atlanta were presented and reviewed with Madeline M. They included the following:

1. The Publicity Kit package and releases.

2. Nineteen small Inventory Binders with appropriate tabs.

3. Ten large binders imprinted for the Accounting Package.

4. One hundred Sales Sheets printed on yellow Day-Glo paper.

5. Photostat of space ad "What do you have to lose?"

6. Typeset sign and easel for "backup" software drawing.

7. Imprinted Trade Show tickets with logo and booth number.

8. Large Software sign with easel for display booth.

9. Patches ordered by Madeline for jackets were picked up and delivered.

10. Art work for calling cards was requested and will be delivered.

11. The proposal for next year's marketing/promotional effort was discussed and the revisions and editions will be presented before final presentation.

12. Lists of retail computer outlets in Atlanta were provided.

Meeting #2: Calibration Division

The following action points were discussed:

1. Vacation Letter was presented to the agency for finalization and printing. This will be produced in a pastel stock ($8\frac{1}{2}''\times 5\frac{1}{2}''$) and the new "Roundup" Data Sheet will be attached. Once printed, this material will be given to Helena for affixing labels and mailing. A total of 1,600 of these pieces will be needed for the Customer Prospect list.

2. The agency reviewed the press conference material that John is to present at the Comdex Show and he commented on the excellence of this material.

3. Material that appeared in *Mini-Micro Systems* magazine (536-7780) was reviewed and the agency is to contact the editor of this publication, Mr. David S., concerning an article and correspondence that John has sent to him.

4. The agency has committed a black-and-white, 1/4-page ad ($3\frac{3}{8}''\times 4\frac{7}{8}''$) in *Mini-Micro Systems* at a cost of $1,723 on a one-time rate. Although this publication will not have extra distribution at the trade show, it will be published in time for the NCC Show. We will have the booth number (#H728) and NCC logo included in this ad. (Note: The sales manager had forgotten that he placed this ad and later this was the only proof that we had his OK to do so.)

5. Previews of next year's marketing/promotional proposal have been discussed with John who has provided input and will review the final version before final presentations.

6. The publicity release on the "Data Rep" company appointment has been released and will be distributed this coming week.

7. The agency is to send a copy of the current ad, which included the NCC trade show logo, to John as soon as it is available.

8. Three of the new "Roundup" Data Sheets were delivered as ordered, along with 3,000 Alignment Cartridge Data Sheets.

Meeting #3: Cassette Division

1. A new Vacation Letter was written and the agency is to produce 200 copies as directed, which Jack will review and have Helena mail on his return from the show.

2. We have discussed various phases of the marketing/promotional proposal and are including input from Jack on various aspects of the market and new customer potential.

3. The agency presented the article, "The Magnetic World of Media," which appeared in the December issue of *Today's Office* magazine. We are to follow up with the editor and see if we can get publicity in the way of clarification of this article under the company's name.

4. Jack was informed that the "Roundup" Data Sheet, which includes "Magnetic Media," was available in printed quantities and can be used with his Vacation Letter.

The Call Report also can be an excellent source of information from your in-house staff; we suggest that you require your staff to submit these reports on a regular basis (weekly or monthly). It will keep them on track and let you know whether or not they are up to date with tasks and responsibilities. Make up your own form for reporting on meetings and *use it*. Try to have others in the organization do the same after every important meeting or phone conference.

BASIC MEDIA TOOLS

There are two very important resources at the communicator's command. *Bacon's Publicity Checker* (see Fig. 1-2) contains complete lists of all type publications and their editors. (We will go into *Bacon's* more thoroughly in Chapter 5.) *SRDS,* published by Standard Rate & Data Service, Inc. (see Fig. 1-3), describes, in detail, practically every publication printed in the United States and Canada, and even publishes a

Figure 1-2. *Bacon's Publicity Checker.* (Used with permission of Bacon's Publishing Company, 332 S. Michigan Avenue, Chicago, IL 60604.)

Figure 1-3. Standard Rate & Data Service (*SRDS*). (Used with permission of Standard Rate & Data Service, Inc., 3004 Glenview Rd., Wilmette, IL 60091.)

volume covering community publications. *SRDS* volumes cover business publications, consumer magazines, newspapers, radio and TV stations, agriculture publications, and even direct response vehicles. In addition to providing rates and discount schedules, *SRDS* provides editorial profiles, circulation, rep contacts, audit information, and publishers' names, addresses, and phone numbers.

Although *SRDS* is an excellent place to start when selecting media, before making any final decisions you will want to contact all the publications you are seriously considering and obtain their "media kit," which will provide more in-depth information (more detailed rate card, demographics, special issues, etc.) on a particular publication.

BASIC LIBRARY

Finally, there are many and varied publications devoted to advertising, sales promotion, marketing, publicity, and the like. By subscribing to and *reading* these publications, you will keep abreast of what is going on in the communications industry—another sure and basic method of becoming a more professional communicator. The following is the beginning of a list of publications that you should start compiling as part of your basic communications library.

Ad Week (212) 529-5500
Advertising Age (312) 649-5200
Business Marketing (312) 649-5260
High Tech Marketing (203) 255-9997
Marketing & Media Decisions (212) 391-2155
Sales & Marketing Management (212) 986-4800
Target Marketing (215) 238-5300

2

Planning
and Budgeting

Everyone agrees that "you can't get there from here" without knowing how to proceed. That is painfully true when trying to implement a communications program. Whether you handle advertising and publicity duties along with a number of other responsibilities, as is true in the case of the small business owner, or you are a full-time advertising manager, thoughtful planning will help you "get there."

At the outset you must determine what your goals are for the next promotional period. This could be for thirteen weeks, six months, a full year, or more. More importantly, you must develop *definite goals*. It is not enough to say, "I want to increase sales in the upcoming year." The increase should be expressed specifically in terms of dollar amounts, or percentages, or numbers of new customers, or some other measurable objective.

Your goals might well take other forms. Here is a representative sampling of common goals in both consumer and industrial advertising:

1. Suggesting additional uses of your product for which many customers and prospects might not be aware.

2. Introducing a new product into your present market.

3. Introducing an established product into a new market.

4. Introducing a new product into a new market.

5. Persuading customers to purchase your product year round, not just on a seasonal basis.

6. Informing customers of significant changes in the channels of distribution you use.

7. Establishing a trade character that you plan to associate with your company or line of products in your promotional material.

8. Developing a cooperative advertising program with your dealers or distributors.

Of course, many other possibilities will present themselves to you based on your particular situation. Regardless of what objective (or objectives) you select, make sure your statement is specific rather than general.

CONTENT OF A MARKETING COMMUNICATIONS PROGRAM

We are frequently tempted to think of our promotional program in terms of advertising messages alone. As we put together our objectives and the manner in which we hope to achieve them, we must remember that there is a lot more in the package than advertisements in newspapers, magazines, radio, and TV. The program embraces publicity, public relations, and sales promotional activities directed at the consumer, the sales force, and the middlemen, as well as direct mail, collateral materials, trade shows, advertising specialties, contests, and on and on. It is important to consider how all these separate areas will work in harmony as we zero in on our goal.

Many of these tasks can be handled in-house by the full- or part-time promotional manager. However, sometimes it is the better part of valor to seek outside counsel. The criteria that are most important in the selection of outside agencies are discussed in some detail in Chapter 11, Parting Shots.

As stated, there are many aspects to any promotional program, but the one you will most likely face first is your mass media advertising program. A comprehensive advertising schedule should carry the following information (see Fig. 2-1):

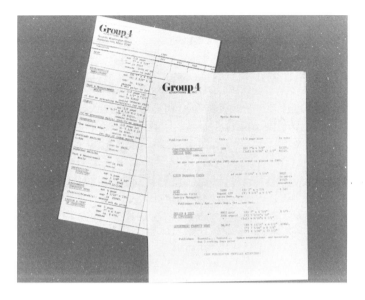

Figure 2-1.   Space schedule.

1. Where the advertisements will run.

2. When the advertisements will run.

3. The cost per ad, per paper, and the total costs for the length of the schedule.

4. Circulation of the publications listed.

Keep in mind that even though you might be running in a score of newspapers, dozens of magazines, and numerous spots on radio or TV, the schedule would be similar—showing where, when, and cost. Once you begin to consider launching an advertising program of even very modest scope, and once the word spreads, as it will, prepare for an invasion of space-and-time salespeople from familiar and unfamiliar media names.

Obviously, you cannot buy from all of them. This means you must become highly selective when building your schedule. Consider the audience of each of the possibilities. Do the media reach the individuals or companies that make up your market targets? Do they reach enough of them? Do they subtly "endorse" your product? Surveys reveal that most subscribers to the *Wall Street Journal* believe the ads as well as the news content of the paper. *Good Housekeeping* guarantees the statements made by its advertisers. As a matter of fact, the Good Housekeeping Seal carries more weight than any other, including the Underwriters' Laboratory Seal of Approval. Advertisers in both these publications benefit from this favorable reader reaction.

You cannot eliminate cost from serious consideration of which media to use. Full-page advertisements in some newspapers can be purchased for $500; others charge $30,000 or more for the same amount of space. Page ads in magazines run from $1,000 to $100,000. Small-town radio stations will sell you a minute of time for $10. A national TV network will charge you $600,000 for a half-minute ad aired during a Super Bowl game.

Costs of using the various media can be found on their rate cards or you can look up the information in the directories published by Standard Rate & Data Service. In the *SRDS* publications (see Chapter 1), you will find all the information you need relevant to costs, circulation figures, and mechanical requirements. (More about this will be discussed in Chapter 7.) Some regional marketing magazines produce inexpensive issues that show charges made by the media in their areas. *New England Media Directory* (see Fig. 2–2), for example, offers an annual compilation of media costs for the six-state area.

Figure 2–2. *New England Media Directory.* (With permission, *New England Media Directory,* 5 Auburn Street, Framingham, MA 01701.)

So, of course, a prime question to be answered in the media selection process is, "Can we afford it?" or "Do we have the bucks to turn to the papers that stack up so well on the other criteria?"

BUILDING THE BUDGET

One of the difficult, but certainly essential, activities you will face is the job of putting together your promotional budget. Organizations take a variety of approaches in arriving at this figure, but two methods are the most used—percentage of sales and sales objectives.

In bygone years many firms preferred to set their budget at a percentage of sales level. Some used a percentage of past period sales but most based their budget on a percentage of predicted sales. If you wish to make use of a percentage of sales, we strongly recommend that you go the predicted (anticipated) sales route.

Becoming increasingly important in the budget-setting process is the method that looks both at the objectives a company has established and then the tasks necessary to accomplish those objectives. If it seems apparent that there will be insufficient monies available, then the objectives should be modified.

For example, a company might set as an objective for the upcoming year that it wants to penetrate the West Coast market. On discovering that the funds do not exist to perform the tasks necessary to do this successfully, the company should probably lower the objective. Maybe the objective should be to enter the greater Los Angeles market rather than the entire coast.

Another method of budget setting is to follow one's major competitor. If that competitor steps up its promotional activity by 5 percent, then the follower does the same. This is none too logical because the two firms might well have different objectives.

Some organizations turn to the "go-for-broke" approach. They scrape together every dollar they can to fund their communications program. If it works, fine. If not, they lock the door. A western Massachusetts company, Adell Chemical, developed a classic marketing triumph thanks to the go-for-broke method way back in 1959. So successful was the operation that Adell became known as the Cinderella company of the fifties. Manufacturers of an all-purpose liquid cleaner called Lestoil, the company had never exceeded $100,000 in sales in any of the previous twenty years of its business life. Yet, after pouring every available dollar into TV commercials in Northeastern markets—a true last-stand effort—Adell's sales skyrocketed to $100,000 per day or $36,000,000 per year. Their chariot did not turn into a pumpkin. This fairly unorthodox method of coming up with an advertising budget paid the richest dividends.

Your task has not ended when you finally arrive at a promotional budget figure. You must then determine what percentage of the total will be allocated to advertising, what percent to sales promotion, and what percent to publicity/public relations. A typical allotment might show 60 percent for media advertising, 20 percent for sales promotion, and 20 percent for public relations. The percentage breakdown will vary in your case, of course, as you decide which of these communication arms will work best for you.

A similar problem presents itself as you make decisions on what percentage of your advertising money will go to specific media categories such as newspapers, magazines, radio, and so on. That problem becomes somewhat more complex as you decide to add additional promotional forces to your arsenal, for example, direct mail and outdoor advertising.

BUDGET USE

Regardless of how many dollars you put in your promotional budget, you cannot do everything you might like to do. Even a big leaguer like Procter & Gamble cannot do all it wants.

There are three major areas to consider when building an advertising schedule: coverage, repetition, and impact. When considering your budget, you must remember that you cannot be involved 100 percent in all three of these areas. Something has to give.

Coverage refers to circulation—how many people read a particular newspaper or magazine, how many listen to a radio or view a TV station, how much traffic passes an outdoor bulletin board, and the like. *Repetition* relates to how frequently your message appears in print or on the airways. *Impact* describes the attention-getting value of a specific advertisement or total campaign.

Every advertiser would like to use every newspaper and magazine covering their particular markets. That certainly would assure them of huge circulation numbers (coverage) but it would also, most assuredly, exhaust even the healthiest budget. Even if a company selected just a few papers and magazines and placed ads in every daily, weekly, or monthly issue of each (repetition), funds would soon be depleted. And, if the advertiser opted for an electrical spectacular outdoor message in Times Square or many two-page, four-color advertisements in costly magazines or two-hour specials on TV (impact), the budget would not last long.

So, in putting together an advertising budget, compromises must be made.

WHICH IS BEST?

You could touch off an interesting argument if you asked a group of seasoned ad people to name the most important technique in advertising: coverage, repetition, or impact.

Much depends on the situation. A company launching a new product line will probably do best by concentrating on impact. A smashing advertisement in any of the media will catch the eye (or ear) of those who are unfamiliar with the new item. Observe the high-impact efforts of the car manufacturers when they introduce the new year's models.

If your product is one that travels through trade channels to reach the ultimate consumer, you can rely on this approach to impress the middlemen important to you. This advertising will help your salespeople sell more effectively when showing your latest products to distributors and retailers.

Impact can also be called upon to promote a special event, such as a mammoth annual sale, a consumer contest, an open house—to name just a few of the many possibilities.

All else being equal, the authors feel that in most instances repetition merits the starring role. The more frequently a prospect sees a message, the more it will motivate that individual to take the action the advertiser wishes him or her to take.

We admit that this is a moot point and that those who favor coverage or impact can develop persuasive arguments to substantiate their choice. After you have built and implemented an experimental number of schedules, you should begin to see a pattern to help choose between coverage, repetition, and impact.

When you have determined the amount of your budget and you have selected the media that you will use, additional decisions still remain. Just as one example with newspaper advertising, you could opt for a schedule of similar-sized ads (for instance, quarter-page ads) for every insertion, or you might feel that a variety of sizes might make for a more interesting campaign. In this case, you might run a half-page ad one week and a one-eighth-page ad the next. Such a schedule should cost about the same as the similar-sized schedule yet would give you more impact with the half-page insertion and would not sacrifice repetition because of the lower-cost one-eighth pages.

When putting a new or updated product on the market, some advertisers make it a point to announce the new item with large ads (two pages) and then keep continuity by following up with small ads (one-eighth pages). Again, the budget figure can be preserved. But now the advertiser enjoys impact along with repetition.

On radio or TV, companies usually air a group of commercials for a particular buying season and then back off for a period of time. This purchasing of a bundle of ads for a relatively short period of time is referred to as *flighting*. Should you make use of the airwaves, you will do better if you make use of a strategic flighting plan.

ROP OR PREFERRED POSITION

The rates quoted by newspapers are called ROP rates, which stands for run of paper. That means that if and when the newspaper accepts your order to place advertising, the paper has only the obligation to print your message on the day you request. The paper controls the placing of the advertisement. It might appear on page 4 or page 68. It might appear at the top of a column or at the bottom of its page. You are assured only of the fact that the ad will be somewhere in the paper on a given day.

If you wish your message to run not only on a specific date but also on a particular page, most newspapers will oblige, but not for the ROP rate. You will be quoted a preferred position charge. Frequently this comes to about 25 percent above the ROP rate. Some of the special pages usually sold by some, but not all, publishers are the front page, pages 2 or 3, the comic strip page, the "Op-Ed" page, the business pages, the sports pages, and the TV listing page.

Readership surveys reveal that the position an ad occupies on a page will increase (or decrease) readership. Should you desire to have your message run top-of-column on the outside of the page (a most desirable spot) you can usually buy this position for an additional 25 percent. But what these "preferred position buys" offer you is the opportunity to run your advertisement where you want it and on the page and day you select. We have found, to our delight, that in many cases an advertiser can get a preferred position simply by requesting it rather than paying for it. To take this approach, you submit to the paper your space order with the comment, "Run at ROP rate. Top-of-column business page urgently requested." In many cases the newspaper will honor your request. There is no guarantee, but oftentimes you will get what you ask for. Another way to fight for good position without paying for it is to have a serious talk with the paper's salesperson who solicits your business. Too few advertisers are concerned about ad positioning so your interest in it prompts the paper to help you when possible.

Magazines present a different preferred position story. Consumer magazines sell the inside front and back covers and the back cover at premium prices. Those are the only preferred position charges they make. Industrial magazines do the same in addition to sometimes selling space on the front cover.

OTHER MEDIA RATE TALK

For many years daily newspapers sold space on the agate line basis. The agate line has no relationship to a line of type but serves only as a unit of measurement. There are 14 agate lines to the column inch. For an ad that measures 5 inches deep by 2 columns wide (a total of 10 column inches), in a paper with a rate of $.12/agate line, the total cost would be $16.80 (140 lines × $.12).

Many newspapers still sell on the basis of the agate line, but more and more, and eventually all, will turn to the SAU. This is the standard advertising unit (one-column inch) in newspapers across the country with uniform column widths. It is much simpler and much more rational.

Weekly newspapers, favorites of small-budget advertisers, have always sold by the column inch and not by the agate line. The major problem with the weeklies is that each one seems to feature a different column width (from 1½ inches to 2½ inches in width).

If weekly papers appear on your ad schedule, be sure you know exactly what size mechanical you should send to each one.

Another interesting phenomenon in the daily newspaper world is the differential rate charged local versus national advertisers. On the average, the local advertiser pays about 40 percent less than the national advertiser for the same amount of space. Like the agate line, this discriminatory pricing is passing from the newspaper scene, but not too rapidly. If you are entitled to the local rate, make sure that you get it. Check with the various salespeople for the newspapers with whom you are doing business.

Both radio and television offer advertisers different rates depending on the time of day (or night) the message is broadcast. The most costly rates reflect the medium's prime time. Radio's prime time runs from about 6:00 to 9:00 A.M. and from 4:00 to 6:30 P.M. TV's prime time includes the hours between 8:00 and 11:00 P.M. On some stations a nonprime-time minute might cost $400; prime rate on the same station could easily be $2,500. A small budget dictates that you go nonprime on TV. When you do this, you must realize you are sacrificing audience size. (More information about the electronic media, including telemarketing, will be presented in Chapter 8.)

POSITIONING

Part of your planning and budgeting task will most likely include a defining process known as *positioning*. One of our clients presented us with an interesting interpretation of the word *positioning* as it applies to the marketing world. His interpretation, commonly voiced by others, is totally incorrect. In his opinion, an example of good positioning was to have his products displayed at eye level in a self-service store or in a display at the end of an aisle.

When professional communicators include positioning in their planning, they are not concerned with the physical location of the goods in a retail establishment. They are concerned with the way that various segments of customers and prospects think about their companies and their products.

What position do they occupy in the minds of these people? This positioning can be established in a couple of ways. First, the marketer may survey the field and discover that certain specific products do not exist. If he or she can develop a product to fill this niche, the individual will engage in positioning. Second, the marketer might take a product that does exist and, through promotional strategy, persuade his or her public to see the product in a new light or in a new position.

A classic case illustrates both of these positioning approaches very nicely. Johnson & Johnson's Baby Shampoo came into the market as a gentle, effective shampoo that did not irritate youngsters' eyes. Such a product did not previously exist. This shampoo was developed to fill a most specific niche. That is positioning.

Then, after the product had become established, Johnson & Johnson's promoted it as the ideal shampoo for grownups, too. Without changing name, formulation, or package, the company redirected the public's thinking about the item. That, too, is positioning. Did it work? Sensationally! Johnson & Johnson's Shampoo became the top-selling brand of all shampoos in the country.

The point of all this is that in your planning process you might well consider whether or not the possibility exists for you to take a new positioning stance that could lead to greater rewards.

UNIQUE SELLING PROPOSITION

Many products offered for sale—in both the industrial and the consumer markets—bear little or no difference from the competition. Thus, in your planning stages you might want to build into your item a desirable feature found in none of the others. Maybe your product can come in a size or a color or at a low price or possess an extra "gizmo" or two that makes it stand out from the crowd. Marketers refer to this feature as a *unique selling proposition* or USP. Most advertisers who have incorporated a USP in their product make sure that they highlight this fact in all of their promotions. Their product stands apart from the various "me, too" competitors. If you can develop a meaningful, unique selling proposition, you have a formidable hook on which to hang your advertising themes. They will almost write themselves.

One medium you do not want to forget when focusing on your USP is your package or its label. Your package provides you with a golden opportunity to ensure that you reinforce the differences you have stressed in your advertising messages. Whether you produce a product for the consumer or the industrial market, you do not want to overlook the importance of your package and package design. Actually, it is one of the really few media over which you have complete control of your advertising. Further, attractive package design costs no more than second-rate design, and it can stimulate your sales significantly. We will concentrate more on packaging when we get to Chapter 4, Sales Promotion/Product Literature/Presentation Materials. The purpose in reflecting on it here is to counsel you to be sure that your USP is prominently featured on your label.

ADVERTISING AGENCY PROPOSALS

You may elect to handle all of your marketing communications programs in-house. We have developed this book to help you do just that. We will talk more about in-house and out-house (oops!) advertising operations later.

On the other hand, as word spreads that you are investing some dollars in promotion (and spread it will), you will be approached by various advertising agencies anxious to work with you.

Whether you make use of outside services or not, you might well base your own planning on a typical proposal format used by an advertising agency when soliciting an account. In other words, do for yourself what you might be tempted to hire others to do for you.

Many agency proposals recommend that the planning for a promotional program start with a marketing audit. Specifically, this attempts to uncover your target markets and to determine the most effective methods of reaching and influencing them. This could include the drawing of a demographic profile of present and potential customers for your various products. Such information is critical to the selection of appropriate messages and media to be used for hard-hitting advertising, public relations, and publicity campaigns.

PRELIMINARY MARKET RESEARCH

Marketing research plays a vital role in making the marketing audit. Both internal and external research will help you come up with the answers to pivotal questions such as:

- What is the company's current market share for each product?
- What is the dollar size of the potential market?
- How effective is the pricing strategy?
- How sensitive is the product to pricing alternatives?
- Is the packaging effective and attractive?
- Are promotional efforts evaluated on a regular basis?
- How are they evaluated?
- What channels of distribution are now used?
- What kinds of communications are set up with your distributors and dealers?
- Who are the competitors?
- What is competition doing, communication wise?
- How are the product lines unique?

In Chapter 1, you received some tips on how to handle your marketing research in an economical fashion. We suggest you review that chapter when you launch your research effort to establish your market audit.

CRITICAL BASICS

The budgeting and planning for your advertising effort will yield rich or meager rewards, depending on a few fundamental requirements. However, these results will be negative, regardless of the caliber of the promotional program, if your product lacks quality, is priced too high, and/or suffers from weak distribution.

The buying public of consumer or industrial goods can be motivated by effective advertising to purchase a weak product (or service) once. Rest assured, however, if the product does not deliver the promised benefits, the dissatisfied customers will never return to it—not when competitive items give them what they want. And no advertising can be developed—even by the gurus of Madison Avenue—that will stimulate repeat sales for that weak product. Thus, we have a basic guideline for a successful campaign: You must have a good product.

Closely related to product quality is package quality. As stated earlier, your package can serve as your most effective advertising medium. Beyond that, it must meet dealer and consumer demands to sell well. Obviously, the package must protect its contents. Few retailers or ultimate consumers will purchase a product in a package that has not protected freshness, fragility, odor, taste, or other important attributes.

Further, the package should be easy to open and reseal and should adapt itself well to the spaces it will occupy. For example, the dealer looks for a package that conserves valuable shelf space—one that stacks well and displays well. If the product is one that the home consumer normally keeps in the bathroom medicine cabinet, then it should fit readily into the cabinet—not too deep, too tall, or too wide.

Let's assume that your product is top drawer. Then, a well-designed advertising campaign cannot fail. Right? Not necessarily. Prospects might be convinced they should make the buying decision, but they do not because the price seems to be excessively high. It is true that you might justify asking a premium price for your product, but there will be a level above which you cannot go because it is too rich for any buyer's pocketbook. Interestingly, it is not always high prices that discourage buyers; unusually low prices can turn people off, too. Since many equate price with quality in their minds, low prices mean low quality.

Even with a "good" product, the "right" price, and motivating promotional material, you can still court disaster. You can do this by neglecting your distribution activities. Some prospective buyers might search for a while as they look for a dealer carrying your item. But if you have such spotty distribution that most of the logical outlets are not covered, even the most motivated individual will purchase an available competitive product. As a matter of fact, your persuasive advertising could well generate a sale for a rival company.

Let's say the copy and illustrations in one of your newspaper ads results in a prospect making a decision to buy your product. Let's also say that your distribution is poor, but to add some sparkle to your ad (to sound much more grand than you really are) you advertise, "On sale at better stores everywhere." Mrs. Jones visits her local department store and seeks out your product. In her mind, her department store is a "better store everywhere." If she cannot find your item there she might purchase a competitive product because your advertising has persuaded her to buy that generic product. Your anemic distribution pattern has let you down.

To summarize, many factors play a role in the budgeting and planning stage. It will be your responsibility to stay on top of all of them or engage individuals or firms to lend you a hand and advice.

But you know where the buck stops, don't you?

TYPICAL PROMOTIONAL PROGRAMS AND BUDGETS

The following promotional plans and budgets represent communications strategies for a variety of products and services with a wide range of dollar allocations targeted to widely diverse markets. Although the budget categories are valid and can be adapted to your particular situation, the dollar values placed may not apply except to give a sense of the proportion of your budget devoted to a given area. Again, this will depend totally on your specific circumstance.

◀——————————————————————————————————

Sample: Promotional Programs and Budgets

Case #1:   Small Payroll Computer Service Company

The overall promotional campaign will extend for a three-month period and will include a space advertising program, a direct mail program, a publicity campaign, a radio campaign, and miscellaneous promotional opportunities as they arise. All costs are approximate.

Space Advertising: The space program will consist of a series of three high-impact ads to be run alternately in the *Nashua Telegraph*. In this daily, we would recommend two insertions per week at a combination (reduced) rate in a $6\frac{7}{16}''$ × $10''$ size (30 column inches) in the Business section. Space costs will run $200 per insertion.

Space costs .... $ 5,000

Production of three black-and-white ads including artwork, typography, and mechanical preparation.

Production costs .... $ 1,500

Direct Mail Campaign: Using the same creative approaches developed for our space ads, the agency will produce two direct mail packages for mailing to target market businesses. Mailing lists will be hand compiled from *The Directory of New England Manufacturers,* Chamber of Commerce materials, and the Yellow Pages. Production costs include printing, list compiling and materials, and postage and handling.

Production costs .... $ 5,000

Publicity Program: A strong corporate identity program will be launched, and the agency will set up and implement a news release campaign for dissemination to all appropriate media.

(Covered under Agency Service Fee) .... N/C
Materials, handling and postage .... $ 500

Radio: Radio Station WSMN reaches the business audience most effectively in the Nashua area. Drive times on this station range from 6:00 to 10:00 A.M. and 3:00 to 7:00 P.M. Cost for sixty-second spots in these preferred times is approximately $18 per spot. We recommend that four commercials be written, and that a special package be purchased to tie into and back up our print promotions.

Time costs .... $ 2,000
Production costs for duplicate tapes,
    announcer, and special effects .... $ 500

Agency Service Fee: @ $1,200/month $3,600

TOTAL $18,100

Case #2: Division of Major Computer Peripheral Equipment Manufacturer

First quarter budget, January, February, and March

Space Advertising: .... $ 9,140

3x . . . *The Office* . . . 1/2 page island
        (4⅝" × 7") @$2,330 $6,990.00
1x . . . *Office Systems* . . . 1/2 page horiz.
        (6⅞" × 4¾") @$2,150   2,150.00
Production of one black-and-white ad including artwork,
typography, and mechanical preparation in
  two sizes   800.00

Publicity: .... $ 2,000

Outside costs (Postage, printing, etc.)

Product Literature: .... $ 7,000

Art and production costs
1. New 4-page, 2-color product brochure $5,000.00
2. Data sheet   1,000.00
3. Reprints of existing literature   1,000.00

Direct Mail: .... $ 3,000

Outside costs only, lists, postage, printing and handling

Direct Response Cards: .... $ 3,400

The Office . . . 2x (Jan. & Mar.) @ $1,400 $2,800.00
Production   600.00

Trade Show: .... $ 3,000

Estimated cost for Show Guide (space) $2,000.00
Exhibit update and ad production   1,000.00

Special Promotional Opportunities: .... $ 3,000

Outside production for collateral materials

TOTAL $30,548

Case #3:   Consumer Program for Legal Services

The following six-month budget recommendation is for use as a guideline to categories and rough cost estimates only. Specific allocations will be made once an actual budget is finalized.

Space Advertising: $15,000

Cost of inserting ads in given publications. (See media selections.)

Production Costs: .... $ 1,200

Cost of preparation of ads including artwork, typography, and mechanical. Three ads @ approximately $400 each.

Newsletter: .... $ 6,000

Cost of writing, editing, and preparing a 4-page newsletter for printing. Published quarterly @ $1,500.

Publicity/Public Relations: .... $ 3,000

Setting up and implementing a continuing program of news release materials for dissemination to editorial contacts in the trade and business press.

Direct Mail: .... $ 2,500

Cost of creating and writing as well as acquiring appropriate mailing lists—ready for postage.

Brochures and Other Collateral Materials: .... $ 5,000

TOTAL $32,700

Case #4:   Introduction of New Regional Publication

The following is a rough estimate of cost allocations for a one-year period.

1. Market Analysis Evaluation:

   This category includes survey charges, consultant fee, and marketing materials costs .... $ 1,200

2. Sales Promotion, Advertising, and Publicity:

   These costs include charges for space advertising, printing and production of direct mail and sales promotional materials, and charges for various agency services $11,000

3. Administrative Costs:

   This category includes additional salaries, office expenses, and overhead .... $ 3,000

4. Product Update and Development:

   This category includes production and printing additions and revisions of the National Drug List .... $ 2,500

   TOTAL $17,700

IN-DEPTH MARKET CHECKLIST

In addition to the general market queries mentioned earlier, we suggest that you try to get some input on the following more complete and detailed company evaluation checklist before you settle down to any specific long- or short-range planning.

The answers to the following questions about your company, its market, products, and direction will provide the kind of information you just have to write a realistic promotional program. Although you may not be able to get a complete set of answers, the more answers you do get, the more practical and effective will be your plan and operational program.

PLANNING/OPERATIONAL QUIZ

- What type of customers buy what type of products?
- What title or job function buys?

- Where are they able to purchase? Where do they purchase? Why do they purchase? When do they purchase? How much do they purchase?

- What is the size of your market?

- Is it growing or declining?

- Who are your competitors?

- What do you know about their marketing program?

- How should the product be positioned?

- What market segments will be most attracted?

- How important are service and warranty?

- Is there a need for product changes or improvements?

- How important is packaging?

- What kind of distribution channels are set up?

- What will best motivate distribution channels to carry the product?

- What pricing policies have been set?

- How vital is price to the sale of the product?

- Has a definite promotional budget been set and verified?

- Have maximum and minimum promotional budgets been evaluated?

- Can you measure the effectiveness of your promotional program tools?

- What media are most effective?

- What copy platform is most effective?

- What publications are most effective?

- What is your company's perceived image?

- Last and most important from your point of view, what is the awareness level to your products, and can it be improved by increasing your promotional efforts? In other words, Is your promotional program as efficient and cost effective as it can be? If not, why not?

OPERATIONAL REQUIREMENTS

Finally, we have included the following list of functions undertaken for various clients under a fee arrangement. We offer it as a guide to most of the activities you will need to include in your planning and budgeting. The list includes many of the basic tasks that you will need performed either internally if you are operating as a house agency or by an outside agency if that is the way you choose to go.

1. A "Marketing Audit" to determine strengths, weaknesses, and objectives in order to prepare a meaningful, cost-effective, and complete communications program.

2. The creation and production of collateral materials, including a corporate facilities (capabilities) brochure, sales sheets, sample cards, and the like.

3. The writing, editing, and distribution of publicity and public relations materials.

4. The steady flow of marketing information and creative promotional ideas.

5. The evaluation and selection of appropriate media.

6. The creation and production of high-impact cost-effective ads for selected media.

7. Development and implementation of a creative direct marketing program (including strong corporate identity program).

8. The development of appropriate compelling trade show exhibits.

9. The identification and evaluation of market targets.

10. The direction and control of any necessary photography, artwork, printing, and all other outside supplier services.

3

Printing
and Production

Printing costs are usually straightforward, and the traditional three-quotation method of comparing costs before selecting the printer is a relatively safe way to make sure you are paying a competitive price for a given printing job.

It is wise, however, to check and sometimes recheck your printer's capabilities, especially when you move from a simple black-and-white job to more complex color printing. When considering new printers, the first step is to look at some samples of their previous work in order to determine if they are capable to meet the standards of your job.

In addition, it is especially important to make sure that all the printers who are to quote a price have received the same job specifications for the job at hand. Be sure that when each quote comes in it covers all the specifications you have indicated. For example, if you are asking for quotations on a full-color job and one printer indicates that he or she will supply a 3M proof but another does not, you should find a discrepancy in cost between the two. Check all the little items on the quote to make sure they conform precisely with one another. Using a standardized form (see Fig. 3-1) for these quotes is advisable.

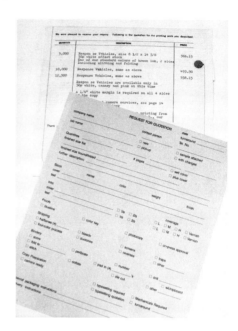

Figure 3-1. Printing quotation information.

THE WONDERFUL WORLD OF GRAPHIC ARTS (SCRATCHING THE SURFACE)

We do not have the space, time, or inclination to go through the entire range of the various printing processes. This would involve a multitude of past, current, and upcoming methods of getting words on paper, including such areas as letter press, rotary press, offset lithography, offset press, web offset, offset duplicators, gravure, screen processing printing, laser printers, and the whole new field of computer desktop publishing. We will leave such research to you, as your need and/or interest dictate.

This also applies to the investigation of the many different kinds of paper stock (sometimes referred to simply as "stock"). Quite a few paper companies and their representatives and brokers will supply you with an abundance of material on the various grades, textures, weights, colors, and styles of their paper. Also, we will not attempt to delve deeply into the area of type, composition, typography, and typesetting, all of which refer to the process of selecting, arranging, and formatting

proofreaders' marks

style of type

wf	Wrong font (size or style of type)
lc	lower case letter
lc	Set in LOWER CASE
C	capital letter
Caps	SET IN capitals
c + lc	Set in lower case with INITIAL CAPITALS
sc	SET IN small capitals
. c + sc	SET IN SMALL CAPITALS with initial capitals
rom.	Set in roman type
ital.	Set in italic type
ital. caps	SET IN ITALIC capitals
lf	Set in lightface type
bf	Set in boldface type
bf ital.	Set in boldface italic
bf caps	Set in boldface CAPITALS
	Superior letter b
	Inferior figure 2

position

⌉	Move to right
⌊	Move to left
ctr	Center
⎵	Lower (letters or words)
⎴	Raise (letters or words)
=	Straighten type (horizontally)
‖	Align type (vertically)
tr	Transpose
tr	Transpose (order letters of or words)

spacing

ld in	Insert lead (space) between lines
ld	Take out lead
⌣	Close up; take out space
#	Close up partly; leave some space
Eq #	Equalize space between words
#	Insert space (or more space)
space out	More space between words

insertion and deletion

the/⟩	Caret (insert marginal addition
δ	Delete (take it out)
δ	Delete and close up
e	Correct letter or word marked
Stet	Let it stand (all matter above dots)

paragraphing

¶	Begin a paragraph
No ¶	No paragraph.
Run in	Run in or run on
flush	No indention

punctuation

(Use caret in text to show point of insertion)

⊙	Insert period
⋏	Insert comma
⊙	Insert colon
;/	Insert semicolon
	Insert quotation marks
	Insert single quotes
	Insert apostrophe
set ?	Insert question mark
!	Insert exclamation point
=/	Insert hyphen
	Insert one-em dash
(/)	Insert parentheses
[/]	Insert brackets

miscellaneous

⊗	Replace broken or imperfect type
⊘	Reverse (upside down type)
sp	Spell out (twenty gr)
Au/?	Query to author
Ed/?	Query to editor
⌐	Mark off or break start new line

Figure 3-2. Standard proofreaders' marks.

words and symbols for reproduction. Basic information on all of the above—printing, type, and paper—are explained in publications provided by several leading paper companies, such as S. D. Warren Company. This firm makes available the "Idea Library," a series of publications that include samples of paper and creative ways to produce various types of printed documents.

BASIC PRODUCTION COMMUNICATION TOOLS

One of the most important ways used to communicate effectively with your printer is to employ standard proofreaders' marks. The symbols shown in Fig. 3-2 represent the generally accepted system of marking changes in your copy and on the proof that your printer will return to you for final approval before printing. Standard proofreaders' marks are also found in the back of most full-size dictionaries.

PANTONE MATCHING SYSTEM®

Another graphic arts communications tool is the PANTONE MATCHING SYSTEM. One component of this system consists of a PANTONE Color Specifier 747XR book which contains color swatches of 747 PANTONE Colors printed on both coated and uncoated paper. Each swatch is identified with a PANTONE Number. (See Fig. 3-3.) The complete PANTONE Color formula is shown beneath each PANTONE Color in the book.

How important is this tool? Well, suppose the president of your company has decided on a formal "corporate color" and the interior decorator has selected just the right hue to reflect the company's warmth and feeling. You could wind up carrying a rust-colored drape to your printer and asking him or her to duplicate that precise color tone on a brochure printed on a glossy stock. (Don't laugh! One of the authors went through this exercise, and it was like trying to carry a bucket of steam to the print shop.) How much simpler and more exact to pull out your handy PANTONE Book and have the decorator choose from the

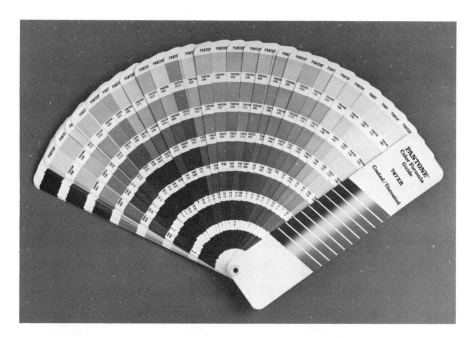

Figure 3–3.   PANTONE® Color Formula Guide 747XR. (Used with permission of Pantone, Inc., 55 Knickerbocker Rd., Moonachie, NJ 07074. PANTONE® is Pantone Inc.'s check-standard trademark for color reproduction and color reproduction materials.)

747 color sections. And since the formula for mixing the ink is right beside the color identification number, your printer has all the information needed to combine the right inks for the perfect match.

PHOTO CONTACT SHEETS

Another convenient production tool or method is the photo contact sheet, also known as the photo proof sheet. This is simply a sheet of photographic paper upon which a roll of film has been printed. The photo contact sheet is an economical method of checking which negatives you like from an entire roll of film. Because the negatives are placed in contact with the printing paper and exposed to light (hence the name contact sheet), the positive prints that result are the same size as the original negatives. (See Fig. 3–4.)

Figure 3–4.   Photo contact sheet.

The proof sheet is extremely useful. It can be used to compare your exposures before you have a final print made, which could be too dark (contrasty) or too light (too little contrast). In addition, the proof sheet provides an excellent means of checking expressions on people's faces, which is impossible to do on the negative. It also provides a handy filing device that lets you easily find a certain picture for later use. It is wise to keep a proof sheet, either color or black and white, with your negatives since it is far easier to distinguish details on the contact proof than on your film negatives. Remember, whether you are taking your own photographs (as discussed in a later chapter) or using a professional photographer, the least expensive item when on a photographic "shoot" is the film. And also remember that you may never have the opportunity to get the same shot again. So, shoot lots of film and make contact prints in order to be able to review from a wide selection of "shots."

STOCK PHOTOGRAPHS

Stock photographs are another valuable time- and cost-saving tool that may help you solve photo production problems. They are pictures that have already been taken and are available on file to be licensed for use or reuse. Stock photos cover a wide range of applications and situations and are catalogued by type of subject—children, senior citizens, buildings, cities, historical sites, factories, models, or just about any subject, situation, or application you can imagine.

One major source for photographs of everything from automobiles to zebras is the American Society of Magazine Photographers (ASMP), which has over 4,200 members and provides an excellent clearing house for off-the-shelf photos. This association also provides a geographic breakdown of photographers who are available for specific assignments. Another stock house that we have found especially accommodating is the H. Armstrong Company, 4203 Locust Street, Philadelphia, PA 19104 (215) 386-6300. This company provides black-and-white prints as well as slides.

A trap you will have to watch for when utilizing stock photographs is that the material may be dated. For example, on one occasion when we needed a computer scene for a low-budget brochure, we chose a photograph for the cover that showed a young woman at an old computer installation, which was unfortunate enough, but even worse we later found out that her hairstyle and clothing suggested a period earlier than we wished to depict.

The PMS color book, photo contact sheets, and stock photos are not the only production shortcuts available. You will find and/or develop many of your own "tools of the trade" as you come up against real-life production problems.

PRODUCTION COSTS

Since printing jobs are quoted in advance and are a well-defined entity, costs for printing are easily determined and can be accurately budgeted. This is not always the case with charges incurred for related production items such as costs for rough or final artwork, mechanical preparation, photography, typography, photostats, client corrections/alterations, newspaper mats, and a host of other production items that go along with producing a given ad or promotional piece. These types of miscellaneous production costs can easily be forgotten and can pop up as most unpleasant and embarrassing surprises. For example, it is difficult to explain a $600 expenditure for duplicate photostats needed to provide varying specifications for different publications when no such cost was considered when budgets were allocated.

Although printing charges are usually the single largest cost in a production budget, many times the small miscellaneous charges can add up to an enormous and, worst of all, *unexpected* cost, and, when laid on top of a well spelled-out budget, these "surprises" can put expenses out of the ballpark. The list of production items in Fig. 3–5 is

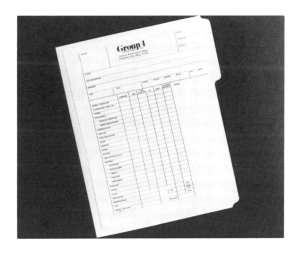

Figure 3–5.   Reproduction of job jacket.

taken from an actual agency "Job Jacket" (the folder that an ad agency uses to track every job and its expenses). Notice, please, that even this list, as complete as it may appear, has a place marked "other." In better than half the jobs in which we have been involved, one or more additional items have had to be added to complete all the extra "chargeables" that went into the particular job. These Job Jacket project categories can serve as a checklist of possible "charge" items and should be consulted when budgetary costs for ads and collateral materials are needed.

TYPES OF PRINTED MATERIALS
(COLLATERAL MATERIALS)

As you review the various types of printed materials in the following list, bear in mind that not only will you have to consider the cost of printing but also the cost of making them ready for camera. (Production costs are sometimes lumped together under the general heading of mechanical preparation.) Should your agency come up with a magnificent full-color, sixteen-page dummy for your new facilities brochure which includes a die cut and embossing, *make sure they provide a "not to exceed" total cost including production and printing.* You may want to get other printing quotes as well, but have the agency quote on printing so both you and they understand what the finished piece is going to do to your overall budget.

COLLATERAL MATERIALS LIST

Since we are on the subject of printing and production and in the area of defining terms, we offer the following list of types of printed materials that we believe you will run into most frequently. Most fall under the heading of "Collateral Materials," which primarily refers to promotional efforts other than media advertising. We are grateful to S. D. Warren Company for permission to use the following:

Annual report: A contracted designation for the annual report of the financial condition of an enterprise. Used to inform stockholders and employees of the financial results and accomplishments of a year of operation. Incorporated occasionally, as a secondary objective, is the use of the Annual Report as a vehicle for general public relations or sales promotion.

Booklet: This word, too, is a designation of form. Booklets are greatly used by commercial enterprises for carrying informative and inspirational messages to customers, employees, and investors. A booklet may contain any number of pages that may be needed to persuade, to demonstrate, or to educate.

Bulletin: This designation is used loosely to describe several forms of printing. It designates the official notice that is posted on a bulletin board in a factory; it designates the periodic factual news report that is sent to salesmen and dealers; it designates the clinical or technical report that is sent to professional or technical men (and women). For the most part, printed bulletins issued by business enterprises consist of sales bulletins and technical bulletins. Generally, a Bulletin is presumed to be one of a sequence of factual reports that will be issued at irregular intervals whenever new information is available. The forms of a bulletin may be single leaf, a folder, or a booklet.

Catalog: This designation is applied to any printed work that presents detailed description of a product or a group of products. There are several classes of catalogs.

Industrial Catalogs: These are ordinarily published for profit by independent publishers, who sell space on their pages to suppliers that serve a particular industry.

Company catalogs: Issued by manufacturing enterprises in their own behalf, these catalogs present only the company's own products. An enterprise that manufactures a variety of products may elect to issue a comprehensive catalog that lists, describes, and illustrates all of its products; or it may elect to issue separate and detailed catalogs for each line of products; or it may choose to issue both the comprehensive and the individual catalogs. Catalogs may also present services as in the case of college catalogs. Most catalogs are in the booklet form. Some large catalogs are bound as books. Some are bound in loose-leaf bindings.

Circular: This is an omnibus designation that is applied loosely to a variety of printed pieces. A circular may be single leaf, a folder, or a booklet of a few pages. A circular may be used to announce any kind of an event, activity, product, or service.

Demonstration or presentation book: This term designates a book or a booklet to be used by salesmen for making illustrated presentations of products, philosophies, and services. Demonstration books are usually designed for presentation to customers in their offices. They are often bound in one of many varieties of ring binder devices.

Envelope enclosure: A leaf or folder or booklet prepared expressly for enclosure with business letters, invoices or monthly statements mailed in the standard commercial correspondence envelopes. Used to remind of products and services or to present selected features of products or services.

Hand bill or flier: This designation is generally applied to a single leaf, printed on one side, for distribution from door to door by hand. The principal usage is for announcing a local sale to the people in the immediate neighborhood, and in political campaigns to promote candidates or issues.

House organ: A house organ (often termed "company publication") is a periodical publication issued by a business enterprise to promote the interests of the enterprise. House organs may be issued expressly for employees or for dealers or for customers. The principal usage of house organs is to evidence the philosophy of the executive management of an enterprise. House organs are issued largely in booklet form; some are designed as magazines; others are styled to resemble newspapers.

Illustrated letters: These are folders of 4 pages and of standard letter size (8½″ × 11″). They are designed to carry a typed, signed letter on the front page and to carry pertinent printed information and illustrations on the inner pages.

Instruction Book: Occasionally a book, more often a booklet, that could also be called a manual. Used to instruct in the operation, care, and repair of mechanical devices; or to teach proper usage of materials.

Mailing card: A mailing card is a single leaf or a folder of Bristol thickness which is sent through the mail to announce an event, to feature a product or service, or to invite some form of response.

Manual: A manual is an informative handbook, reference book, or guide. Manuals may be issued for customers, employees, or salesmen. Employee manuals generally explain shop practices, employee obligations, privileges, and benefits. Salesmen's manuals are intended to equip salesmen to find proper answers for all pertinent quesions regarding their company or its products or its services. Manuals for customers usually present technical instructions for the effective operation and maintenance of mechanical devices. Manuals are widely used today in industry and government to instruct or educate in complex technical fields. Manuals are generally in the booklet form.

Package enclosure: A leaf, folder, or booklet to be enclosed in a package of merchandise. Used primarily to instruct in proper or advantageous use of the product contained in the package; used also to draw attention to companion products.

Pamphlet: This designation is one of form and is generally used interchangeable with the term "booklet." Among some groups, the word "pamphlet" is used to designate a minor booklet of few pages.

Poster: A single leaf or paper or card that is printed only on the face and that is to be posted in a public place. Used to present brief messages to those who may read in passing.

Return card: A single leaf of Bristol thickness enclosed in a mailing to serve as a return post card for the convenience of readers who may wish to respond to an offer.

PRODUCING A PROMOTION: START TO FINISH

Now that we have overwhelmed you with the multitudinous kinds of collateral materials that you are most likely to encounter, let's now take a look at where it all starts and how we wind up with a final promotional piece.

Although much of the following brainstorming session could have been placed in Chapter 10, The Creative Effort, we decided to run through it here in order to show the flow that takes place in getting from the original concept to the final production stage and the printing of a brochure (or placing an ad, or mailing the direct mail letter, or whatever). For us, no matter what type of promotional avenue we may take (collateral materials, space, radio, TV, or direct mail) the methodology is usually the same—and it all starts with the central idea or theme and winds up with the final production of the piece.

The following session took place shortly after a meeting in which the authors, Ed McGee and Bob Cox, were assigned the task of creating and producing the sales promotion and advertising for a large Chrysler auto dealership. The initial creative session included Ed McGee, who represented the marketing viewpoint; Bob Cox, the senior copywriter;

and Maris Platais, who was the agency art director. It went something like this:

Bob: Ed, I'd like to ask you just what your overall impressions were on the client meeting the other day and get a feeling of how we should position him and what unique selling proposition we can find to set him above his competition.

Ed: I don't see any specific advantage like price, quality, delivery, or even service with a big enough difference that this dealer can push above his competition. To me, it looks like we'll have to look for an emotional appeal rather than a specific competitive advantage.

Bob: Well, there was one thing that seemed to come through to me, and that was that this client's automobile agency is really an extension of the owner's own personality.

Maris: Maybe we can get on track here as far as the art is concerned. Suppose we use a cartoon caricature of the owner the same way we used photographs of other clients who were not only company owners but also were perceived and identified as the company itself.

Bob: That's an excellent idea! This man has built his automobile agency single handed, and it will please him to be its representative trademark as well as its owner.

Ed: It is also appropriate for the public to view him as the agency spokesman as well as its owner. This way we personalize the operation and present the top man as the one you will deal with as a customer.

Bob: OK then, what we need is a central strong and appealing theme line and, since we are going for an owner/company identification, let's see what the man himself has that his public will find appealing and memorable.

Ed: Well, we know that he is golfer and has a full-scale putting green in front of his dealership.

Bob: That's right! That would appeal to customers since he mentioned that he was invited to the Bob Hope Golf Classic, and the subject of golf came up several times in our initial meeting.

Maris: That would be an easy one from an art standpoint, especially if we go to a caricature of the individual as a golf pro.

Bob: That's the word—*pro*—How about a line like, "It pays to know the auto pro"? It has rhyme; it ties to the professional

Ed:	in golf; and it establishes him as the leader in the automobile agency business.
Ed:	Sounds good to me. What do you think about the art, Maris?
Maris:	From the photos I have, he shows up as a fairly attractive guy, and I'm sure I can work up some roughs with a flattering caricature in a golf hat with a club. It'll make a nice logo.
Bob:	Let's go with it! I'll get going on some initial headlines and rough body copy to fit into your rough art. OK with you, Ed?
Ed:	Sounds great!

This is the way the initial brainstorming session went and how the central theme was established for that particular auto agency.

The next step in this process was the creation of some rough art sketches that centered on the caricature of the owner with a golf club and a golf hat with the letter *B* and the tag line, "It pays to know the auto pro."

From this "working rough" concept stage, which sometimes consists of a copywriter using stick figures, we proceeded to tighten the visuals and included typeset headlines to produce a "comprehensive rough" for presentation to the client. In this case the client enthusiastically approved the comprehensive art and typewritten copy, so we then moved to the actual production of the ad and began creating other promotional (collateral) materials based on the same theme. (See Fig. 3–6.)

After first approval (the art usually goes smoothly but the typed copy can take some time because the client often agonizes over every word), we proceeded to what is known as the "mechanical stage" where type was selected and set, and the entire piece was made "ready for camera."

Once again, a presentation was made to the client for final approval on type selection and final art touches. After final approval, a "safety photostat" was prepared and sent off to the printer. (In some cases the safety photostat is sent to the publisher depending upon whether we are working with an ad or collateral piece.)

This, of course, is an oversimplification of the actual production process, which can involve a range of technical functions such as screening photographs, producing a Velox, viewing proofs or blue

Figure 3–6. Rough art approaches through final mechanical artwork. (Used with permission of Bournival World of Transportation, 831 Rogers St., Lowell, MA 01852.)

lines, approving 3M color proofs, making sure that it fits the mechanical requirements of the given publication (if it is an ad), and a wide range of other functions that are best left to the artist and/or printer to perform.

To recap:

- Everything starts with the concept.

- Next comes the rough art, layouts, headline treatments, and sometimes a copy platform (general line copy is to follow).

- This is followed by the comprehensive layout or complete view of the art and finished headlines, along with polished typewritten copy.

- Then comes the final mechanical preparation, which includes all finished and approved elements assembled on a bristol board and "shot" (made into a printing plate) by the printer. This stage includes all production processes that we have discussed in this chapter but with which you will probably never become directly involved.

In the case of the promotional program for this particular auto dealer, we first produced an introduction ad that explained the who, what, when, and why of the "Auto Pro." After the space ads, we proceeded to the production of all kinds of collateral materials, including license plates, brochures, and a range of ad specialties, each with its own set of production problems and each carrying the swinging golf pro logo, and the central message with which we started.

PLACING AND TRACKING PUBLICATION ADVERTISING

One last activity, which is related to production, is the placing and the keeping track of ads in the chosen publications. In the larger agencies, this task falls to the Traffic Department. This department directs all photostats, ready-for-camera artwork, negatives, and the like to the appropriate publications. This phase of production also includes checking that the varying mechanical requirements of each publication have been met and that each specification is correct. Also at this stage insertion orders are issued and space schedules are maintained. (See Fig. 2–1.)

All of the information on the space schedule, such as dates and frequency of insertions, size, closing date, type and name of ad, and so on, now must be communicated to each publication. This is done by means of an insertion order, which is a contract between the advertiser (or his or her agent) and the salesperson to run the space on the day requested and for the amount specified. (See Fig. 3–7.)

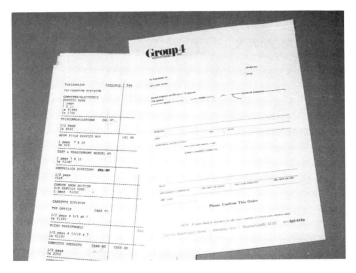

Figure 3–7. Insertion order form.

4

Sales Promotion, Product Literature, and Presentation Materials

The three topics discussed in this chapter, sales promotion, product literature, and presentation materials, represent fundamental activities and are significant enough to include separately on any budget sheet.

I. SALES PROMOTION

This is one of those nice general, catchall categories that can include just about any promotional activity that does not happen to have a specific label. Sales promotion is a great place to locate all kinds of miscellaneous areas without using the word *miscellaneous* (an anathema in budget planning). Space advertising, publicity, direct mail, trade shows, and the like are pretty well defined, however, the sales promotion category is not so specific and thus provides a place for all kinds of promotions that do not quite fit a regular budget category.

SALES PROMOTION AREAS

The items on the following checklist are arbitrary selections of miscellaneous promotional items, most of which you will probably have to consider somewhere along the line. Hopefully, this partial list will prove useful as a reminder of some type of promotion you might neglect at budget planning time. Here, then, is a wide range of materials and activities encompassing the broad field of Sales Promotion.

Ad Inquiry Referral Forms
Advertising Specialties
Annual Reports
Application Guidelines
Association Speeches
Billing Forms
Buyers' Guides
Calling Cards
Catalogs
Company Logo
Competitive Cross References
Competitive Intelligence Forms
Competitive Product Evaluations
Complaint Report Forms
Customer Lists
Distributor Contracts
Distributor Policy Manuals
Envelopes
Factory Tours
Final Test Reports
Headquarters Contact List
Installation Drawings
Installation Instructions
Kits/Lists
Letterheads
Maintenance Instructions
Manufacturers' Representative
  Lists
Manufacturers' Representative
  Contracts

Market Surveys
Nameplates
Open House
Operating Manuals
Order Acknowledgments
Performance Specifications
  Sheets
Point of Sale Aids
Price & Discount Sheets
Product Announcements
Product Bulletins
Prospects Mailing Lists
Quality Control Tests
Quotation Forms
Reprints—Ads & Articles
Returned Goods Policy
Returned Goods Tags
Sales Awards
Sales Meetings
Sales Policy Manuals
Sales Territory Maps
Samples
Shipping Cartons
Shipping Labels
Slide Presentations
Spare Parts
Stock & Shipment Sheets
Specification Sheets
Terms & Conditions of Sale
Trade Journal Articles

User Lists   Yellow Page Listings
Warranty Policies

You will, of course, be adding to this list with your own particular items. The important point here is that you have a checklist to which you may refer at budget time and, at that time, you will have the opportunity to include such items specifically or set up a budget category to contain such expenditures. We also suggest when you budget that you set up a contingency fund to take advantage of promotional opportunities that will arise during the course of any given year and for which there is no way to plan. These opportunities can include such efforts as presenting papers at trade symposia, conducting open house and other community relations projects, operating award functions, and purchasing various types of advertising specialties.

Sales promotional activities also include a constant study of cartons, packages, and labels from the viewpoint of appearance, better use, easy recognition, and the overall image of the company. You also have to prepare manuals, instruction sheets, inserts, and tags, as well as installation data that goes with the product. All of this is part of sales promotion.

Promotional activities for the sales department include writing sales letters, new customer letters, and letters to former customers (clients); analyzing sales records; planning demonstrations in the field; corresponding with the company salespeople and their dealers, as well as jobbers, and wholesaler salespeople; checking on daily inquiries; preparing for trade shows and exhibits; arranging for samples and demonstration displays; handling trade shows and association meetings; planning, writing, and making detailed arrangements for talks and speeches given by the company and sales personnel; assisting with sales training; designing the special displays and exhibits for schools and college educational use; and so on.

Your sales promotional program has a serious responsibility to the sales manager and must be designed to help reps, jobbers, and wholesale distributors, as well as your own salespeople. The rep's, jobber's, and wholesaler's salespeople must be sold on the company's products, services, and its advertising, promotion, and merchandising efforts. These vital distribution groups must be educated on how to use the sales, promotional, and merchandising material furnished by you in order to obtain more business.

PACKAGING: DRESSING UP TO WIN

Packaging is sometimes a neglected promotional medium. When you have your sales promotion hat on, you should keep an eye on all packages, cartons, shipping cases, and labels, from the standpoint of the company's image. All packaged goods should tell the user in a flash the pertinent data required. A little field use or on-the-job investigation will give you the answers to many of your packaging needs. Talk with the counter-people, the mechanics, the warehouse people—whatever individuals handle your merchandise—and each of them will tell you what he or she needs in order to best sell your product on a daily basis.

Instruction sheets, manuals, tags, or inserts should be included with all package goods. Use short, clean, and to-the-point copy. Illustrate your instructions with sketches. Clarity and simplicity are the order of the day, as instruction sheets are referred to many times in the field.

Regardless of whether your package goods or your service require instructional data, be sure to insert a piece of literature promoting your other products or services in which customers might have a possible interest. They may not know that you offer these products or services as well as the ones they generally purchase. Don't forget: *Your current customer is very often your best prospect.*

SAMPLE SALES PROMOTION BUDGET

The following sales promotion budget was developed several years ago for a new product called "The Buttoneer"—a five-second button attacher. It includes only collateral materials (in this case, supplemental printed promotional materials). See Figure 4-1. Each item and the quantity required were listed as printing quotes were received.

◄───

Sample: Sales Promotion Budget

Figure 4-1. Buttoneer kit. (Used wtih permission of Dennison Manufacturing Company, 275 Wyman St., Waltham, MA 02154.)

Memo to: Marketing Director

From: Advertising Manager

Subject: Anticipated Buttoneer Collateral Materials Budget (intro period)

    1. REPRINT ITEMS   PRINTING COSTS
      a. Sales Kit Covers (2M) $ _____
      b. Ad manager Kit Envelopes (2M)
      c. Ad Reprints (2M ea. of 3)
      d. Merchandising Sheet (2M)
      e. Publicity Montage (2M)
      f. News Release (Letterheads)
      g. Advertising Mats (2M)
      h. TV Storyboards (2) (2M)
      i. Two-Color Bill Stuffers (10M)
      j. Refill Order Forms (5M)
      k. Glossry Product Photos (2M ea. of 3)
      l. Radio Script Reprints (2M)
                     TOTAL PRINTING COST $ _____

2. REVISED MATERIALS CHECKLIST
The following is a list of the literature we are planning to revise with anticipated costs to produce and print in order to bring these pieces up to date. Both production and printing costs are estimated.

EST.
PRODUCTION
AND
PRINTING COSTS

a. Merchandising Sheet—1 page, 2-color (5M) $ _____
b. Publicity Montage—1 page, 2-color (2M)
c. Full Color TV Storyboard for New Commercial (2M)
d. Two Color Bill Stuffer—4 pages, 2-color (2M)
e. New "How To Use Buttoneer" Booklet—8 pages,
   2 color (2M)

3. NEW MATERIALS SALES PROMOTIONAL BUDGET
Various pieces of promotional literature also will be required for the several new market areas that we contemplate entering. Although it is difficult to estimate accurately the cost of new promotional pieces that have not yet been finalized, we have indicated some rough figures that anticipate costs for these entirely new materials.

a. Brochure directed to industrial market plus   EST. COST
   one or two supplemental pieces $ _____
b. Promotional and backup literature for serviceman's kit
c. Literature and promotional material for men's travel kit
d. Chart and literature for home economics promotion
e. Brochure for Dry Cleaning Campaign

TOTAL $ _____

4. ADDITIONAL BUDGET CONSIDERATIONS
Although the Buttoneer Instruction Booklet is not ordinarily considered a promotional piece, we have on several occasions used it to supplement our regular promotional literature; therefore, we have estimated costs for revising and printing this particular piece for promotional purposes.

Full-color, 12 pages, self-cover. Printing Approx. Booklet (250M). Anticipated costs for layout, copy, artwork, etc.

$ _____

In addition to the literature listed here, there will be about a dozen forms (cooperative advertising sheet, reorder forms, etc.) that will be produced internally and for which no budget has been allocated.

Sincerely,

---►

PROMOTING TO THE SALES FORCE

No discussion of sales promotion would be complete without including the most important target of all—the sales force. Certainly, sales contests, quotas, trips, prizes, and so on all have value, but in our opinion solid lines of communication through sales letters, meetings, trips to the field, and the like are more useful for keeping the sales force involved and motivated over the long term and on a continuing basis. This is especially true of the communication of sales leads and inquiry follow-up programs, as discussed in Chapter 1.

One of the most important ingredients of any promotional program is the input of the sales function. It is most wise to get your own internal salespeople as well as your reps and/or distributors involved before you get too far along with any promotion. This accomplishes two goals: First, because of their field experience, these individuals can warn you of pitfalls; and second, it makes them a party to and, therefore, supportive of the final result.

A CENTRAL THEME

It is most desirable to have a central theme running throughout a particular sales promotion campaign and, wherever possible, coordinate that theme with other promotions.

As with most of your efforts, success in one area depends on how well you are able to coordinate it with all other areas of your overall program. This is especially important when making up a promotional kit for your sales personnel or rep organization.

For example, a theme line such as "Five-Second Button Attacher," with its "product in hand" artwork can be used in direct mail programs, ads, advertising specialties, posters, display pieces, outdoor advertising, and the like. Sometimes a theme can be carried throughout with a simple art device incorporated into the logo, such as the twin circles used for a cow embryo transfer service. (See Fig. 4-2.)

Figure 4-2. Simple art device depicting central theme.

Remember, too, that your production costs will be lessened through this kind of coordination since the same artwork, sometimes modified slightly, can be used in a wide range of different programs.

Discussed next are a few proven sales promotional devices that you may want to consider to improve communications with your various channels of distribution.

Internal House Organs

Among other benefits, a regular newsletter (internal or external house organ) directed to the sales organization is a most powerful promotional tool. Internal house organs and external newsletters are both excellent sales promotional tools. They are the ideal vehicles to keep your in-field salespeople informed of your activities and a great method of getting feedback on your various promotional ideas in the early stages.

Sales Incentive Contests

In our opinion, sales contests have a built-in trap. The goal is to have all of your salespeople work a little harder in order to win the prizes. However, oftentimes, salespeople know that they have very little chance of winning and will disregard the contest entirely and work at a normal pace.

Prizes for achieving a certain quota is another version of the sales contest broadened out to a larger number of salespeople.

The trouble with most sales contests, in our view, is that they do not motivate all of the salespeople. In fact, contests can have a detrimental effect by turning up more losers than prize winners, which can be demoralizing to the entire sales force.

Promotions to Acquire Distribution Channels

As always, before any promotion in any area can be undertaken, the first step is to identify and understand the target market. *Know your audience.*

All promotions to specific market segments, especially those directed toward improving product distribution, should be initiated with an in-field trip to several potential customers. This will provide a clearer understanding of the kind of material that will influence that kind of prospect.

For example, we once had a client who came up with a new product designed to keep small gasoline engines, such as those used in lawn mowers, from running out of oil. The product consisted of a clear plastic reservoir that held a supply of oil and a tube that allowed oil to flow from the extra source into the crankcase as needed.

The major target audience for this product was the automotive after market, where auto accessories not found on original equipment are sold. In order to determine what kind of promotions would appeal to this specific audience, we went out and made calls with the company salespeople and determined that major prospects in this market were automotive product supply outlets. The buying influences were men in the thirty- to forty-year-old range who, for the most part, were quite interested in sports activities.

The object of our game was to reach and obtain sales interviews with major automotive distributors. It was imperative that we make a most dramatic impact among the largest of these auto distributors with our introductory direct mail campaign. The main obstacle to overcome was the reluctance of the busy distributor to set aside time for our salesperson's in-person call.

We finally designed a direct mail campaign that involved mailing a single boxing glove and an accompanying note that said, "The salesperson would like to interview you with a hard-hitting product, and if you can meet with him, he will bring along the second boxing glove as a premium for you." This program was extremely successful and produced an 80 percent interview rate.

COMPANY ANNIVERSARY

The idea of a company making a big splash about being around for many years may not move customers or prospects, but it can provide a possible media opportunity. (See Chapter 5 for some tips in utilizing this type of opportunity.) However, more value will probably be gained from the increased "esprit de corps," not only among your salespeople, but from all company employees. Remember—you do not have to hit the exact anniversary date. It can be when the founders first met, or whenever, as long as it comes out to a nice even anniversary year. We had great success with a company that we estimated was seventy-five years old (diamond anniversary) and were able to incorporate a diamond shape into all their promotional materials and space ads. This improved their logo immensely and gave us the opportunity to use the tag line under the logo, "Seventy-five years of excellence."

OTHER TYPES OF SALES PROMOTIONAL ACTIVITIES

Literally thousands of successful sales promotional ideas are available in various books, checklists, and periodicals on the subject. Your sales promotion effort will be limited only by the stretch of your imagination.

There are two additional concepts in this area that you may wish to consider: cooperative (or co-op) advertising and regional editions of national publications.

Cooperative advertising is simply an allocation or allowance of funds for advertising that a supplier (usually a manufacturer) makes available to a seller (usually a retailer) to help promote the supplier's product. Although this usually involves a product manufacturer cooperating with a retail operation, it can sometimes be provided by a vendor of raw materials to a manufacturer of finished products.

Cooperative advertising funds offer retailers a palatable method of increasing their total advertising effort. Most product manufacturer co-op programs reimburse retailers for around 50 percent of advertising costs and require that the retailer provide evidence of the particular advertising used. Manufacturers will usually include some stipulations as to what will appear in an ad, radio copy, direct mail brochure, or whatever. This will usually include requirements for the use of the manufacturer's logo and name prominently displayed in the promotional effort. The best way to initiate a cooperative advertising program is to approach your largest suppliers and find out how much, and in what period, cooperative advertising funds are available.

The following is a letter from the ad manager of a carpet manufacturer requesting that his company be included in the cooperative advertising of a major materials supplier.

◀────────────────────────────────────

Sample: Request for Cooperative Advertising

Dear (Personalized):

We are most enthusiastic about participating in your cooperative advertising program and know that our company will make an important contribution to your promotional efforts.

We sincerely believe, and will so state, that your firm provides the ONLY materials that can produce the truly static-dissipative, nongenerating, guaranteed, computer-grade carpet and tile required in today's electronic office.

We will also provide dramatic application stories and photos that will testify to the aesthetic as well as the technical advantages of your product over any other materials.

Incidentally, we have just made a major investment in five new carpet lines that boast the exclusive use of your product. Extensive promotion of these lines will target the Designer, Architect, and Facilities

Manager; and a major focus will be placed on today's automated office.

We are hopeful of sharing these kinds of themes with you in a cooperative effort in three major promotional areas. A new product brochure, currently in the design stage, will feature high-tone application photos. This piece would include a prominent display of your logo and full reference to the benefits derived from the use of your product. The cost for this four-page, full-color brochure (similar to the one enclosed) is budgeted at $20,000 for 20M pieces.

The second category that seems ideal for a cooperative effort is the publication advertising program that we are currently developing. We plan to run full-page, full-color ads in such publications as *Architectural Record, Interior Design, Facilities & Design Management,* and *Contract.* Our space program has been budgeted at $60,000, including both space and production costs.

Finally, in the area of Architects' Folders, we will be updating and reprinting folders for our five new lines and propose to include your company and logo prominently in copy treatments.

We believe that we can make the kind of strong statement that only a long-term, totally satisfied user can provide and join in a cost-effective, high-impact program that will work to our mutual advantage.

Perhaps it need not be said, but no copy, art, or anything promotional that relates to your company will be released without your company's full knowledge and final OK.

Looking forward to your thinking on this effort.

Sincerely,

The use of regional editions of national publications is another great way to gain enormous prestige without staggering costs. Many consumer and newsweekly magazines, such as *Time, Business Week,* and others, offer regional editions (editions that go to local metro areas only) in which space can be purchased at considerably less cost than the national edition rate. Check the space representatives of particular publications in which you are interested and ask if their publications offer regional breakdowns of national circulation. Distributing such "national" publications to selected customers, prospects, and reps can be a very effective sales promotional ploy.

While you are at it, also ask what other kinds of promotional or merchandising aids their publications provide. Such items as laminated copies of your ad, the use of a reprinted cover of the publication as a cover sheet for your ad in a direct mail piece, extra reprints, and a range of other special extras may be yours for the asking or at minimum cost.

II. PRODUCT LITERATURE

As we launch into the vital area of product literature, we must issue a warning about delaying your sales effort until the perfect promotional piece is produced. This is particularly important with new ventures. We have seen new firms get hung up on producing the company brochure and almost go broke while everyone waited for someone to create the final masterpiece. It is almost always better to go with a less-than-perfect brochure, or even a preliminary data sheet, and get things off the ground than it is to wait. You can always go back and refine whatever brochure you first produce and, most likely, you will want to make changes and improvements as you get into your market anyway.

The first, and usually the only, impression most customers have about the firms with which they do business is that which is provided by the company's product literature—product brochures, data sheets, price sheets, catalog sheets, flyers, display pieces, facilities brochures, annual reports, and the like.

Product literature describing product characteristics (features) and spelling out product advantages for the customer (benefits) is by far your most important promotional tool. And, while it should be developed first to set the tone for other promotional areas, it is often completely overlooked until a trade show deadline when the sales manager asks, "What the hell are we going to give out at our exhibit?"

Designing and producing effective product literature should get top priority for any consumer, industrial, or technical product. This also applies to a service where oftentimes the only tangible may be a descriptive flyer or brochure.

Product literature is one of the basic and best ways to promote any product or service. It takes many forms, ranging from a single black-and-white specification sheet to a multicolor, multipage brochure.

A solid product, corporate, or facilities brochure is the foundation of any good promotional program. In almost every instance, the message presented by a brochure is the message that persists over time—far more so than the fleeting impression of, say, an ad or a mailer. Also, the brochure often becomes the major vehicle through which a salesperson makes a presentation. For these reasons, the story told by a brochure must be carefully thought out and well presented.

Here are a few of the major functions of a good brochure:

1. Oftentimes a brochure is the first point of substantial contact for a customer beyond the salesperson. As such, it must portray the image of class or sophistication or high tech that the company wishes to project.

2. Brochures are the best presentation tool for a salesperson when he or she has an audience of only one or two customers. In that case, it is more effective than a slide or the use of overheads.

3. Brochures are also an extremely good tool for educating your own sales force as well as your prospects and customers.

4. A new brochure always gives the salesperson another reason for a customer visit.

5. A new brochure provides an opportunity for a publicity release to the new literature section of appropriate publications.

6. Brochures are excellent leave-behind material after a presentation.

7. If they are not too expensive, brochures can also serve as handouts at local trade shows and as response material to inquiries received from PR, direct mail, or bingo cards (response from magazine ads).

MAKING THE BROCHURE

All brochures should begin with a short one- or two-paragraph "executive summary" of the contents. This will provide a good review for the salesperson and customers and will save the time of customers who are not interested in reading further. They will appreciate it and that is actually good business.

Right from the start, it is best if you tie all your literature together graphically. Although the object of graphic design, in the minds of some marketing directors at least, is to create something new and different, it is best to overcome the "all-new idea" temptation. Continuity in the message and look throughout all promotional material will prove of more lasting value than farfetched attempts at being different.

This is not to say that you cannot add variety as you go along. After all, if you have twenty different products, not all of them can be presented in exactly the same format, nor should they. But little things such as the positioning of the company logo on the cover or an unusual typeface or a particular illustration technique can do the job of maintaining continuity.

A seemingly small point, but one that can be rather vital to some customers and prospects, is to design your brochures so that they can be three-hole punched (even if you do not punch them). There has never been a time in the history of brochures when some customers or salespeople did not want to three-hole punch them and put them in a notebook. It would be unfortunate if they hole-punched through the most important part of your text or the most meaningful portion of your photograph or illustration.

WHERE TO START

How do you start any fundamental piece of promotional material? Well, you begin with the basics. (Once again, back to Chapter 1.) Whether you write and design your own sales literature or hire professionals, the first thing to do is to determine exactly what the material is to contain and what you hope it will accomplish. One of the best ways to do this is to create a strategy sheet and ask yourself questions such as the following:

- What should this brochure accomplish?
- What product or service is being offered in this brochure?
- Who are my competitors and what are their advantages and disadvantages?

- What are my company's strengths for this product or service?

Next, define the audience:

- At what level or sophistication is this brochure aimed (company presidents, department heads, actual users of the product, or whomever)?
- How will a product or a service help this potential customer?
- What are the major areas and points that need to be covered?
- How will I use this brochure? How many copies will I need? What is my total budget, including writing, photography, art preparation, and printing?

Save your strategy sheet for future reference. You will need it, whether you write the brochure yourself or employ a professional to do so.

How can you find a free-lance copywriter? Many writers advertise—look in the Yellow Pages or read the ads in local advertising publications. (Most metropolitan areas have a weekly or monthly publication that keeps their advertising and public relations community up to date.) One of the very best ways is to do a little networking among your peers and ask other companies for recommendations. You can investigate local advertising agencies that handle literature as well as advertising and put a small ad in a local newspaper for a free-lance writer with some experience in your field.

What should you look for in a writer? Ask to see the writer's portfolio and check whether he or she has the ability to develop your specifications and to carry them through in the brochures. In particular, make sure that the individual has some experience in your field. The writer must be able to understand how your product or service works and what its advantages are before he or she can convince anyone else of either of these things. If a particular piece that the writer has done intrigues you, find out how he or she arrived at that.

What do you need to give the writer? Show the writer your strategy sheet and discuss it in depth. He or she must know your budget, target audience, and what you expect the brochure to accomplish. Explain what size brochure you are looking for in general so that the individual can schedule his or her time and have some notion of charges. Having samples of other companies' literature that you particularly care for will help the writer understand what you are trying to achieve, and they will provide a basis of discussion about what you like or dislike.

What can you expect from the writer? Based on your requirements and deadlines, the writer should quote you a price. Some writers quote by the job; others quote an hourly or daily rate. Ask him or her to submit an outline of the projected brochure complete with titles and section headlines. A good brochure always has a theme, and headlines and titles carry the reader through and reinforce this theme.

What if you don't like what you get from the writer? Tell him or her what is wrong—whether it's the tone, approach, or technical information. You have final approval and that gives you the right to make suggestions and corrections. Do not blame the writer for any mistakes or changes of mind on your part, however. Remember—each writer uses an individual style to meet his or her objectives, so don't quibble over words or sentence structure.

What if you want to do it yourself and write and produce your own literature? The first thing to do is look at your strategy sheet, especially your target audience. If you want to reach data professional personnel, for instance, you will want to write about your product or service in computer-related terms. If you want to reach nontechnical decision makers, you will describe your product advantages in everyday language. It is best to create an outline, decide how much information you want to cover, and determine the sections into which you want it divided. Generally, it is a good idea to start with a brief company background, explaining how and why you started what you are doing. For example, if you have a software package for accountants, you should mention that someone in your organization worked as an accountant and thus knows an accountant's business problems first hand.

Remember that readers like to read copy that is benefit oriented. Always spell out to the audience what the product or service will actually do for them. It is not enough to just list the business functions handled by a system or a piece of equipment; it is best to give a brief description of each function using, whenever possible, the buzzwords commonly used within your target audience or market. It helps the reader believe that you understand the business.

The organization of your brochure can be the easiest or the hardest part of the job. Some brochures actually organize themselves. For example, if your product is used on various types of steel mill machinery, you would logically have sections on how it is used for plate mills, coilers, levelers, or whatever specific application applies.

WRITING THE BROCHURE

Most brochures have to be organized along the same lines as advertising copy. This means presenting product features according to how they benefit the reader. A brochure on electric motors, for instance, might begin with how the motors provide more capacity and less space, followed by such factors as built-in protection against overloads and low voltage, features that reduce maintenance and other failures, features that make the motors easy to install, and then a section on how to select the right motor for your needs.

A person writing an ad is hopeful that some percentage of the audience will read all the way through his or her masterpiece. When you are writing a sales brochure, there is hardly any hope of that being the case. Most readers skim through brochures, glancing at the headlines, subheads, pictures, and captions, but reading only a paragraph here and there. The reader will stop and read a section thoroughly only if he or she has an immediate interest in the subject discussed or in that particular use. Isn't that the way almost all of us read brochures? By realizing that this is the case, we can reach a number of conclusions. First, the main story should be told by the headlines, subheads, and picture captions so that even the skimmer will get the whole gist of your message. A great effort should be made to pull the readers from the headlines into the subheads and into the pilot copy, which should be very specific and factual and never general and vague.

Where possible, points should be backed up with a case history, specific tests, installation results, and pay-off explanations of the features you have called out in the headlines.

Good sales brochures rely heavily on pictures, both to tell a story and to make the brochure more interesting. Photographs are usually preferred to drawings, except where a drawing could show something that a photograph can't (exploded views for example). If possible, photographs should be large and squared up, not outlined or tricky. Retouching is sometimes necessary, but if it has to be done, it should be done as realistically as possible.

Charts and graphs should be as simple as possible. Some artists, by an intelligent use of shadings and colors, are able to make charts very interesting, intelligible, and attractive. Most readers know that solid pages of type present a very formidable appearance to the eye, thus practically every page should contain at least one illustration for the sake of readability and interest.

Long text should be broken into paragraphs with frequent subheads. This not only makes the page look more attractive, but the subheads will carry along the reader's interest in the subject matter. Spot illustrations and little thumbnail sketches are other good devices for livening up a page and animating the message.

LAYOUT AND DESIGN

Let's now consider the layout and art preparation stages. There are two ways to prepare your brochure's artwork—hire a professional or do it yourself. Because art preparation is more complex than writing, it is often best to employ a professional at some stage. How do you find this expert? If you have hired a writer, ask him or her (writers are almost always aligned with some designer and they work well as a team), or consult the Yellow Pages, or, once again, ask other companies for recommendations.

What should you look for in a designer? Ask for the designer's portfolio and look at the way he or she artistically develops the themes of other brochures. Be sure to inquire as to his or her experience with local printers because you will need a printer. The designer should be able to help you with the recommendation and should be able to handle this aspect of the job. Designers almost always know which printers have certain types of presses, good paper supplies, and reasonable prices.

COMMUNICATING TO THE DESIGNER

Tell the designer what your total budget is. Budget is often the single most important factor in deciding whether your brochure is to be two or four colors, the quality of paper to be used, the number of copies to make, and if it is to include drawings. Tell the designer what general size you have in mind and give him or her a draft of the copy if it is already completed, or talk about the theme, the audience, and the purpose. This information helps the designer use his or her imagination in creating ways of expressing the theme. It also helps determine type-faces, headline sizes, and other visual factors.

Once again, have samples of other companies' brochures available so that you can discuss what you like or dislike about layouts, photos, headlines, and so on.

What do you expect from the designer? Based on your requirements and deadlines, the designer should be able to quote a price. You can expect a flat rate for the job instead of an hourly rate. There can be certain imprecision in the pricing because the designer can only estimate, for example, how much typesetting will cost.

The first thing you get from your designer will be some thumbnail sketches, which are also called copywriters' roughs. (See Fig. 4-3.)

Figure 4-3. Copywriter's roughs.

These quick, pencil designs on tissue paper can show you how the designer wants to arrange copy, photos, and drawings. Examine the thumbnails closely to make sure the brochure's design has the feel that you want. Thumbnails are relatively fast and easy to draw, and you can freely make suggestions to the designer and expect all sorts of changes at this stage. Especially make certain that the designer has followed the theme throughout with the headlines, designs, and visuals.

After you have approved the thumbnail sketches, your designer will next submit a full "comp" or comprehensive. This is a brochure designed either in miniature or actual size with a very finished look.

The comprehensive layout (comp) will enable you to see the designer's ideas for the cover, how the copy will fit in type, and where headlines, photos, and drawings will fall on each page. You should also get color samples of the paper and the typography that is recommended at this stage.

What if you don't like the design? If the comp doesn't look right to you, ask to see the thumbnails again. It is just possible that you may have forgotten what you had approved earlier. If the comp is significantly different from the thumbnail, then determine whether it is a matter of design or substance. Should the comp be wrong in terms of company image or audience, explain exactly what you feel needs to be corrected. Be specific. Use competitive literature to illustrate points you find hard to verbalize. Remember, though, if you make significant changes in directions at this point, it is only reasonable to expect to pay extra for a second comp.

What about photographs? If you or someone in your organization has worked in photography, at least semi-professionally, you may want to save money and take your own photos. Under no circumstance, however, should you work with an amateur who is touted as having a "good eye with a camera." Discuss with your designer what each photo should contain and the importance of each photo.

For instance, you may want a photo of your company's current facilities. (Not an outside shot of the plant with the flag, please.) This may be important, especially if your company is relatively new and you wish to show the degree of prominence and substance you have obtained.

Usually, your most important picture will be the one of your system or product. Again, the question of budget determines if the photos are to be black and white or color. Film is inexpensive, thus we strongly advise that the photographs be taken in color *and* black and white, whether you are going to use them in the brochure or not. Also, while you are at it, you should have slides made, as they may be very helpful in future sales presentations and other uses.

How do you set up a photo session? Show the designer in advance where you want the photos taken, then he or she should attend the photo session to show the comprehensive layout to the photographer. The two individuals should work closely together to make certain that all photos that are going to be needed are taken at the same time, and also to be sure to get some dramatic angles and unusual appearances.

Make sure the photographer understands in advance the number of photos to be taken, their use, and the content of each. Check that there is no clutter in the area being photographed, waste baskets and ashtrays are clean, telephone cords and wires are hidden, papers are arranged relatively neatly and efficiently on desks, and coffee cups, dishes, and unnecessary mementos are removed. But also be careful not to make the environment overly antiseptic.

If you plan to use people in your photos, and most times that is a plus, there is no reason you cannot use people in your organization as models. However, notify them well in advance so that they will dress neatly and present the image you want of the company. Make sure that the employees understand that they are to do what the designer and photographer want. It is also very important that *whoever appears in a photograph signs a photo release form.*

III. SALES PRESENTATION MATERIALS

Sales materials for use by salespeople when making calls have been termed the "the forgotten media" because once the sales brochure and mass promotion have been given, management often assumes it has provided all the essentials the salespeople require for in-field selling. This is not the case.

Special sales aids and presentation materials should be produced specifically to tell your sales or service story (or both) to your own staff, jobbers, wholesalers, and rep organization. A sales story well told will always bear repeating; therefore, do not hesitate to tell it again and again to your established distributors and their sales force. There are many avenues available to you in the preparation of your presentation. It can be as simple as a chalk talk, or it can be filmstrips, slides, black-and-white transparencies, overheads, movies, or video presentations.

If you are just beginning to develop presentation sales materials for your company, we suggest that you make an effort to use the same media throughout. For example, if you start out with a slide presentation, keep slides for as many different presentations as possible. This will afford you the flexibility of moving parts of one presentation to another and mixing and matching to suit individual audiences.

Many salespeople, especially the most experienced, are reluctant to use canned material. Point out to them the value of having the message delivered to all audiences in a consistent manner with all benefits and features included. However, even though you prepare a written script for them, allow your salespeople the freedom to enhance the material in their own way. Remember, at the start, to keep slides and other types of sales tools you adopt modular so that the salespeople can tailor them to their own audience and style.

The following is a general introduction to a rather elaborate twenty-minute video presentation used by a manufacturer of anti-static carpeting.

◀─────────────────────────────────────

Sample: Introduction Copy for Video Sales Presentation

United Technical Products has developed the following *elementary* presentation on static to introduce you to some very basic and—hopefully—helpful information on electrostatic phenomena.

Everyone knows the discomfort caused by a sudden static zap.

Here, we will show—**in a nontechnical way**—why this occurs and—more importantly—how disruptive, and sometimes destructive, it can be to computers and other static-sensitive equipment used in today's modern office.

We hope this information will help solve any static problems that you may face—and that you will consider the *"Computer Grade"* anti-static floor coverings and other static-protective products produced by **UTP—the static control people.**

─────────────────────────────────────▶

IN-FIELD SALES PROMOTIONS/DEMONSTRATIONS

Sales promotional materials for use in the field are the most valuable contributions you can make to the sales force. Field demonstrations are among the strongest selling tools available because the customer can see the product in use and under simulated-use circumstances. If your product or service is amenable to this "here's how" technique, use it as widely as possible. Many aggressive organizations use demonstration trucks, complete with product displays, which they take to the customer's place of business. Although it seems like a high initial investment, research has shown that it pays off handsomely.

As we will indicate in Chapter 9, exhibits at trade and association shows provide a means for you to show your products and to meet with potential customers in a casual manner and—very importantly—to place your company's name with a large group of buyers in association with other top manufacturers. Oftentimes, display elements from your exhibit, used on major sales calls, can be extremely effective educational displays. Likewise, educational displays are welcomed by many institutions and prove to be an excellent image-building device as well as sales promotion aid when your product or service is showcased as an item of general public interest.

Your function as a promotional person is to serve as the right arm of the sales department. Sales promotional materials can be a constant service to them.

Many larger firms have found it desirable to set up an independent audio visual (AV) department solely to care for their needs for sales presentation materials. It will be worth your while to read up on this important field in texts and publications devoted exclusively to this area, such as *Audio Visual Communications* and *AV Video*.

5

Publicity

PR is a term that often is used to describe both publicity and public relations, but for our purposes here we will concern ourselves mainly with publicity. Publicity is yet another method of communicating *your* particular message to *your* particular audience. And, by the way, it is among the most economical and effective methods of getting your company name or your product/service out in front of the public and keeping it there in a positive way.

Ordinarily, you do not have to pay for the time and the space used in your publicity program, however, there are costs involved, and this important aspect of your program should be budgeted carefully and adequately.

To be really productive, your publicity program has to be well-managed and consistent. Although it is only one aspect of your marketing communications program, it is an extremely important one. It can open doors and favorably affect sales. An effective long-term publicity program provides a cumulative, rather than an immediate, result. It is totally unrealistic to expect your telephone to start jumping off the hook or your sales to double simply because you have mailed out a press release. In the long run, however, it is the stuff from which successful companies are made.

WHEN DO YOU RELEASE SOMETHING TO THE MEDIA?

Simple! Anytime that you have anything that you feel is newsworthy is probably a good time to release such material. Use a bit of discretion, of course. Beware of the impulsive mistake of many tyros who flood the media with a mountain of trivia. For the most part you can figure that something is newsworthy if it stirs up significant in-house interest. However, don't expect that every release you send out is going to be picked up and used on page one of the *New York Times.* Remember that there are literally hundreds of people, companies, institutions, and causes that are also trying to get the same free space and time for their own use.

There is very little that does more to build up good will for your operation than having your customers' or your employees' names and/ or photos in the newspaper. But, for the sake of your Dun & Bradstreet, make sure that you spell each name correctly. Spell it wrong and you will have forever lost a friend or, even worse, a job.

HOW DO YOU PREPARE A PRESS RELEASE?

The first thing to remember is that your press release should be typewritten and double spaced. Every release that goes out must have the name, title, address, and telephone number of the contact person in your shop. The contact person would be the individual who is best qualified to answer whatever questions the editor might have about anything contained in your release. Information about the contact person should be placed at the top of the first page of the release:

FOR FURTHER INFORMATION, CONTACT:
Carlin Walsh, Marketing Director
Viking Mfg. Co., Inc.
22 Chestnut Street
Boston, MA 01567
617/555-1234, Ext. 567

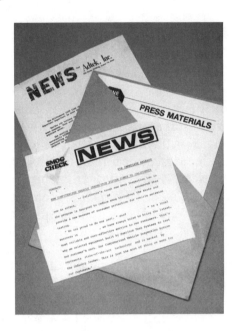

Figure 5-1. Sample publicity releases.

Every release that goes out should have a "RELEASE DATE" prominently displayed at the top of the release. Usually it appears at the left hand margin. It is typed in upper-case letters and can be underscored for additional emphasis. (See Fig. 5-1.)

FOR RELEASE: FEBRUARY 1, 19--

Use of a particular release date is important when you want to have the information contained in your release break into print on a specific date, for example, the day that your sales department is ready to introduce a new product.

If you do not have a specific release date in mind for the item, then the release should be headed:

FOR IMMEDIATE RELEASE:

The use of the release date is an important element of every press release you issue because it provides the editor with the most opportune time to use it. Editors will respect your release date. Often, an item not "deadlined" for a particular date will be used a few days after it is received. Speaking of editors, remember that they are people. Start compiling an accurate list of media people. (We will talk more about how to compile that list later.) Try to have every envelope addressed to an editor *by name*. A personalized envelope is much more likely to be opened and read. You know how you feel about the mail that you get at home addressed to "Occupant" or "Resident." You read these last and usually just scan them before tossing them away.

WHAT GOES INTO YOUR PRESS RELEASE?

A press release is not the place for subjective, personal, or editorialized statements. A good press release is factual and objective. Remember the five W's. Take a good look—they will come up again:

WHO?
WHAT?
WHERE?
WHEN?
WHY?

Who sold it? *What* was sold? *Where* was it sold? *When* was it sold? *Why* was it sold?

> John Jones (*who*) today (*when*) sold a Mini-Mite Computer (*what*) to the town of Swampwater (*where*). The all-transistor computer, manufactured by the Mini-Mite Corporation of Houston, is especially designed to streamline all facets of smaller town operations (*why*).

The sentences in your press release should be brief and to the point. This is not the place for long, rambling, complex, verbose, enriching, medieval (get the point?) prose. If you want some excellent examples of the finest use of short sentences, carefully read the newspaper columnists in any major daily, especially papers like the *New York Times* and the *Wall Street Journal*.

The key sentence in your press release is the first sentence. It must be dramatic enough to arrest the eye and grab the attention of the person reading it—much the same as the headline of a space ad has to be a "grabber," as we will see in Chapter 10. If that first sentence does not capture the eye and pique the interest of the editor, you probably will not make it into print. It will be advantageous to develop a glossary of descriptive "action words." Bear in mind that scores and scores of press releases cross the desk of every editor every day. You've got to get him or her with that opener. For example:

> A revolutionary new communications product for more effective law enforcement has been developed by the Mini-Mite Corporation of Houston, designed to . . . a breakthrough . . . never before possible, etc., etc.

Writing press releases is like any other aspect of marketing. The more often you do it, the more proficient you will become. Your writing skills will improve with practice. (There we go on writing again. You just can't escape it. Promise yourself to read one good book on basic writing as soon as you finish this one.)

HOW LONG SHOULD YOUR PRESS RELEASE BE?

Never use more than two typewritten, double-spaced pages for your press release. If it runs longer than that, get out your blue pencil and edit it down to size. The two-page maximum length is recommended for several reasons. First of all, anything longer will probably not be read. The editor simply does not have the time. Second, the newspaper may not have that much space available. The shorter releases stand a much better chance of being printed. Third, a good press release writer ought to be able to tell his or her whole story in no more than two pages.

REPRODUCTION OF YOUR PRESS RELEASE

Your releases can be photocopied, mimeographed, or reproduced any way you wish. The important thing is to make absolutely certain that every copy you send out is clearly legible. A faint or illegible release will be discarded regardless of how good the story is.

DISTRIBUTION OF YOUR PRESS RELEASE

Even if you produce the greatest press release ever put together, it will not do a scintilla of good unless you get it into the right hands. Distribution of your material is equally important as the creation of it. It is to your great advantage to compile and constantly update an accurate and complete mailing/distribution list of publications and their current editors. Again, remember what was said before about including the editor's name in your list. The finest resource for compiling a mailing list is *Bacon's Publicity Checker,* which is updated several times each year. It contains complete and accurate descriptions of just about every newspaper and magazine published in the United States and Canada. You can order a copy by writing to: *Bacon's Publicity Checker,* 332 South Michigan, Chicago, IL 60604.

Your own "publication/editor" distribution list should be divided into various categories, including:

Local daily newspapers
Local weekly newspapers
Daily newspapers with national or regional circulations such as:
    The *Christian Science Monitor*
    The *Wall Street Journal*
    USA Today
    The *New York Times*
Magazines of general interest
Magazines of special interest
Trade publications
Professional journals

Once you have developed your distribution list, we recommend that you employ discretion (a synonym for common sense) in using it. A strictly local interest news item should not be sent out to publications with a national or international circulation. Similarly, a highly technical or complex item about a purely scientific or theoretical idea should go to the appropriate professional or trade journal since it would be too difficult to comprehend to be useful in a general interest publication. In other words, every press release should not automatically be sent out for mass distribution. The quickest way to lose credibility is to mass mail a release to your entire list. The temptation to do this has increased with the use of the "Mail Merge" function provided by computers.

The thinking that goes, "It's already written and it only costs postage, so mail it to everyone" is not at all smart. *Be judicious with your release mailings.*

It would be well worth your time, and it is practically necessary for any real success, to make the acquaintance of the local editors and trade press people. (In many instances, they need your material as much as you need to have it printed.) If you are placing space, get to know the publication's representative. There is no better way to know your market as well as the opportunity of getting an introduction to the publication's editor.

Another benefit provided by *Bacon's Publicity Checker* is that it tells you the type of release that a given publication will accept for consideration (e.g., new product, personnel changes, trade literature, general news, events, etc.).

Depending on the size of your budget, you might want to consider using a clipping service. This is the best way of keeping track of how well you are doing at getting into print. Clipping services are usually about 75 percent efficient; that is, they will send you approximately three out of every four releases that appear in print. Most of the services have a flat fee for a minimum number of monthly clips and a per-clip charge for each one over the minimum. Use of a clipping service is a particularly good idea if your publicity efforts are national in scope.

In suggesting various categories for your distribution list, the first item in the list is local weekly newspapers. These are an excellent resource for every publicity person. Weeklies are, of course, primarily interested in news about people and events in their immediate, localized circulation area. A release identifying one of your company's employees as a local resident and doing something even relatively newsworthy is almost always certain of getting published. Weekly newspapers rely heavily on unsolicited press releases. For the most part, they do not have the budget or the resource to have a full-time reporting staff.

Our second category, daily newspapers, sometimes publish "regional editions." These usually involve a combination of world, national, and local news. The local news printed covers a particular section of their entire circulation area. They often have local reporters ("stringers") who get paid by the column inch for their contributions. These reporters will welcome your releases and are your best bet for getting your material used. Some digging and research on your part will give you a pretty good insight into what local papers will print. Look for bylines and make a note of the names of reporters who have written stories related to the area in which you are working. Sometimes a release sent to the right reporter can develop into a feature story. As soon as you are able, take an editor or reporter to lunch; you will find that it can be an education in itself. Yet another channel of distribution for your publicity is the wire services (United Press International and Associated Press). You can become a member of these news bureaus or you can have a PR service organization handle the wire services for you.

PHOTOGRAPHS

The old Chinese proverb about a picture being worth a thousand words was never more true than in the case of product or company publicity. Few people cannot help but look at a picture when it appears in a newspaper or magazine, and most will read the caption under the picture.

If you have had limited experience with a camera, don't be dismayed. Spend some time carefully studying the photos that appear in your daily newspaper. Examine how the photos are laid out. Talk to professional photographers and ask their advice and opinions about techniques. Many of them will be delighted to share their expertise, especially if there is a possibility of a later assignment. Your local advertising club or the Yellow Pages can provide you with names of commercial photographers who can give you advice or handle the necessary photographic work for you.

If there are people in your photograph, try to keep the maximum number to three or four. "Crowd photos" require too much space to print a caption and the faces are reduced to such a small size that the people are unrecognizable. If you are taking photos of people, have them *doing* something—presenting a plaque, signing an order, pressing a button, cutting a ribbon—anything to introduce action into the shot.

Try to achieve some sort of balance in the arrangement of the picture. Do not have everyone crowded into a corner with only a potted plant in the rest of the space. The more effort you put into creating an attractive photograph, the better the chances of it being printed. If you are using people in a picture to be released to the media, you *must* have each person appearing in the photograph sign a release or permission form giving you and your employer permission to use the photograph without recompense. Packages of release forms are available at many photo supply stores. See Figure 5–2 for an example of such a form.

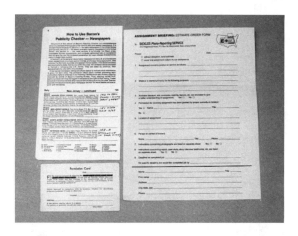

Figure 5–2. (Left) Editorial data in *Bacon's Publicity Checker.* (Used with permission of Bacon's Publishing Company, 332 S. Michigan Avenue, Chicago, IL 60604.) (Right) Assignment form for Sickles Photo-Reporting Service. (Below) Standard Permission card for publicity release. (Used with permission of Sickles Photo-Reporting Service, PO Box 98, Maplewood, NJ 07040.)

◀──

Sample: Photo Release Form

Short Version

Date: _____
I hereby give my persmission to the Goodhue Furniture Corporation of Atlanta to use this photograph in the news media without any recompense to me.
Name: _____
Signature: _____
Address: _____
If person signing is a minor, the parent or guardian should also sign:

_____
(Guardian)

Legal Version

For the express purpose of relieving _____
Corporation of Seattle, WA of any and all liability which otherwise
might arise under any law relating to the unauthorized use of names,
portraits, or pictures, I hereby consent to the use by said company of
the name picture and/or portrait of _____ ,
hereto annexed in connection with its business, whether for advertising
purposes, purposes of trade, or otherwise.

Signed: _____

If person signing is a minor, the parent or guardian should also sign:

_____

(Guardian)

_____ ►

This release should be signed and dated by the individual or individuals appearing in the picture.

If you are distributing photographs of a product then it should be
the focal point of the picture. Try to make the photo as dramatic and
interesting as you possibly can. If at all possible, the product should
be shown in action. Remember—as beautiful or functional or utilitar-
ian as you may see your product, your picture *must* show it. Use your
imagination, throw in a dash of showmanship, and you will come up
with a good usable product shot.

PHOTO SIZE

There are two standard sizes for photographs submitted for publication: 8″ × 10″ and 5″ × 7″. Submitting a larger size does not assure
you of having a larger picture printed.

All publications have the capability of reducing or enlarging all
photographs to fit the amount of space they can make available. We
have personally had better success using the 8″ × 10″ size when the
picture was of people, and the 5″ × 7″ when the picture was of a
product.

MAILING TIPS

When you are mailing your photos, be sure to insert a piece of stiff cardboard into the envelope to prevent the picture from being bent or creased. The cardboard should be approximately the same size as the photo. Be sure to mark the outside of the envelope clearly with the legend: Photograph—Please Do Not Bend.

Any photo you send out for publication should be clear and sharp. *Do not write on the back of photographs* and especially do not write on the back of them with a ballpoint pen; it will show through when (or if) the picture is used. If it is absolutely necessary to mark on the photo, use a soft grease pencil and a light touch.

Do not ask or expect to have any photos you submit returned. The magazines and newspapers simply are not set up to do this. Also, publications do not like to use any "doctored" photos—that is, photos that have been air brushed or mechanically altered in any way. They prefer straight photographs that tell a simple, straightforward story.

Most publications are in the *news* business. They publish the news that they feel is of interest to their particular readership. You and your photographs should respect that basic tenet and cooperate with it.

DISTRIBUTION OF PHOTOGRAPHS

Once again, we recommend the use of *Bacon's Publicity Checker* to develop the optimum distribution list for your photographs. *Bacon's* is coded to tell you which publications will accept photographs. (See Fig. 5-2.) It will also tell you which publications will accept photos of new products.

In developing your mailing list for publicity photos, a little homework on your part will reap unexpected dividends. Make it a practice to read as many local newspapers as you can get your hands on. Look them over carefully and, in all probability, you will find a pattern for the use of publicity photos. Some newspapers will use several photos in the same issue if it happens to be a slow news day. Some papers use them only in certain sections of the paper (the business pages, for example). Some will use only those that have a local tie-in.

Once again, do not overlook those small weekly newspapers (they are, by the way, probably read more carefully and more completely than the metropolitan daily).

There is a story told about three restaurants that illustrates this point very well. All three restaurants were located in the same block. The first owner promotes his establishment with the line, "We have the best cup of coffee in the state." The second puts up a sign stating, "We have the best cup of coffee in the country." The third simply posts a note in the window, "Best cup of coffee on the block." Keep the local approach for the local media. A picture in a limited circulation weekly can sometimes have more direct impact than one that appears in a remote large circulation daily newspaper. Remember that the small weekly wants the local tie-in to a local person or a local company.

An obvious, but sometimes overlooked, place to utilize your photos is the in-house newsletter. (We will talk more about internal house organs in Chapter 10, The Creative Effort.) Please understand that it is most important that the people in your own company know what is going on. It is also a great morale booster for people to know and to see that the company recognizes their efforts and/or their products and/or their contributions to the overall effort. It can also help foster a healthy spirit of competition that can benefit the company. A good public relations gesture is to make sure that every person who appears in any photo you distribute for publication gets his or her own personal copy of the photograph. It also complies with the idea of compensating them for allowing the use of their photo.

PHOTOGRAPH CAPTIONS

The caption you write for your publicity photos should be brief and to the point; remember, it is a picture caption only, not the news release. Simply tell, in a few brief sentences, who is in the picture and what they are doing. You do not have to write clever headlines for your photo captions. The publications have picture editors who are specialists in doing that kind of thing. Refer back to the original five W's when preparing your caption: Who? What? Where? When? Why?

Always identify the people in the photograph. Identifications are usually listed from left to right as you are looking at the picture. For example:

John Jones, Chairman of the Board of Selectmen of Southport,
CA, presses the button to start operating the new Webster Computer recently purchased by the town. Looking on with approval
are (l to r) Frank Smith, Chief of the Southport Police Department, and Diane Laird, President of the Webster Computer Corporation of San Diego, manufacturers of the unique computer.
The Webster can be programmed to handle a variety of municipal
operations, including maintenance programs for police and fire
vehicles, as well as the payrolls for the entire municipal employee
force. Use of the computer is expected to save the town $8,000.00
per year.

Once you have written your caption and had the necessary number
of copies reproduced, the caption then should be taped to the back of
each photo, preferably with masking or removable tape. There should
be about two inches of blank space at the top of the caption sheet. It
should be attached to each picture in such a way that the entire wording
of the caption appears below the photo. (See Fig. 5-3.)

Do not try to type the caption on the back of the picture or paste
or glue the caption over the entire back of the photo, and, again, do

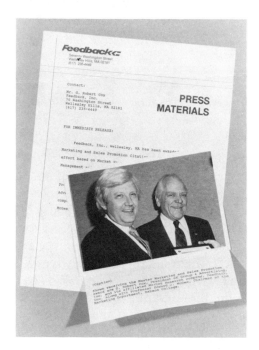

Figure 5-3. Attaching photo captions.

not write on the back of the photo—any of these will damage the picture and make it unusable. Nor should you use paper clips on photos.

It will pay you to learn a little about the photographic process: If you spend some time in a photo lab and learn about such things as contact sheets, cropping, retouching, and so on, you will find yourself way ahead when you go on an actual "shoot" with your photographer.

Photography is an area where you will have to do some shopping around and experimenting with vendors. It is probably the one place your budget can be hurt the most unless you really compare prices. If you look in the Yellow Pages of your telephone book under "Photo Finishing," you will find a long list of firms that can supply you with quantities of publicity photos. A few things to remember when negotiating with these companies are:

Cost per copy
Quality of each copy
Dependability of service
Ability to meet tight deadlines

Remember, you don't have to be a professional photographer, but some working knowledge will be most helpful, and you can pick up pointers and trade jargon from the lab and photographer you do work with on a regular basis. Perhaps you will choose a different photographer for different specialties—the photographer you will use for straight product shots probably will not be the same one you will want to use to photograph a fashion model. Bear in mind that when you ask for a price from photographers and photo labs, you should let them know what size ($5'' \times 7''$ or $8'' \times 10''$) prints you will be looking for, whether you need black-and-white or color, what camera format (35mm, $3'' \times 5''$, etc.) and, in general, the time you think it is going to take and the kind of shot you are looking for.

Remember—do not go to an amateur or try to take your own shots, unless you feel you could make your living as a professional photographer. Keep in mind that you usually get only one photo opportunity and, if you blow it, there goes your chance to have a photo for your release.

If you are interested in getting additional mileage from your press releases, consider distributing them to your local radio stations. Although the smaller local stations may not have the "reach" or large audience that the larger metropolitan stations have, they do have a broadcast day to fill and they want to broadcast items of local interest.

People listen to local stations' news broadcasts because they are interested in hearing about "who and what" is happening in their own area. You can develop your own list of radio stations by checking in the white pages of your phone book under *W* (principally in the East) and under *K* (in the West). Call all the stations in your area, find out the name of the news director and include him or her on your mailing list. Studies and surveys have shown that there is always an audience listening to any radio station on the air. If your release is used, it will be heard.

IT IS NEVER MARKETING VS. PUBLICITY

Your publicity efforts should be tailored to complement and reinforce your overall marketing strategies. If your periodic review shows your marketing strategy to be weak in certain areas, you can address that weakness with a slight "slant" or "spin" (emphasis shift) in your publicity program. If sales of a particular product are down in a specific geographic area, you can shift the emphasis of your publicity program to that particular section.

There is yet another service available to help in this area of publicity support for the sales effort. This is the Photo Reporting Network Service, which is set up to provide you with photographs, photojournalists, and reporters on location throughout the United States and in foreign countries. This service also provides you with testimonials and case-history reports about people, products, and services, wherever and whatever, you desire. The Photo Reporting Service is particularly beneficial in getting the material you need on a product application story, for example, at a far distant site.

The following directions were given to a Photo Reporting Service for a case history (photos and written report) on a client's product installed at a facility in St. Paul, MN. (See Fig. 5-2.)

Sample: Copy for Photo Service Assignment

Dear Mr. Sickles:

If possible we would like to obtain a testimonial account on our client, "COMPU-CARPET," in eliminating static disruptions where previous carpeting (obtain competitor's name, if possible) had to be removed because it did not dissipate a static charge and was responsible for equipment failure.

We would like four to six photographs from various angles at the installations with heavy emphasis on the carpet but also showing static sensitive equipment.

Sincerely,

▶

WHERE DO YOU GET IDEAS FOR PRESS RELEASES AND OTHER PUBLICITY?

There are two basic sources for press release input: people and products. Some sources are obvious: the installation of a new corporate officer, the appointment of a new management-level executive, the design and production of new and exciting products, a major redesign of an already successful product, and so on. If you have built up any kind of rapport with others in the firm, they will often make helpful suggestions on which you will be able to capitalize. Once you use an idea supplied by someone else, you will be surprised by the additional helpful input you will receive. When people find out that their suggestions are not falling on deaf ears, they are delighted to offer constructive ideas. Stay alert for other possible tie-ins. Maybe "National Pickle Week" is coming up and your research department is on the verge of developing a computer that will remove the warts from pickles—that's newsworthy (also a little silly).

Perhaps one of your people gets elected to an office in an organization in which he or she is active—the Chamber of Commerce, Knights of Columbus, American Legion, and so on. That's a press release opportunity. Maybe someone in your organization comes up with a new application for an old product—the kind of application that your competitors have never thought of—that's news, not earth shaking to be sure, but news nonetheless. These are just a few possibilities that show how and why an open, creative mind, constantly alert to story opportunities, is the best source of publicity stories.

Indeed, the extent of your publicity program is limited only by your imagination and the amount of time you are willing to devote to thinking about it.

HOW TO ORGANIZE YOUR PUBLICITY PROGRAM

If you do not have both short- and long-range goals for your program, it may become fragmented and ineffectual. That's what we meant earlier when we were talking about a scattered, hit-or-miss approach. A basic goal of your program might be to create a climate for marketing a new product that will be introduced within a few weeks. Another immediate goal might be set after discussion with the personnel director who indicates that a small problem exists in employee relations. Now, the task could be an attempt to improve morale and motivation among the work force and to inspire them to a more dedicated mind-set. In other words, you must first identify the goal, then try to establish a reasonable and viable mechanism to attain that goal.

You plan your publicity campaign as carefully as you plan any other element of your communications program. You establish priorities, identify problem areas, decide on a specific course of action, develop the means to carry it out, and then, *do it.* You sit at the typewriter or word processor and write your press release. You get the publicity photos taken and reproduced. You get the captions written. You get the envelopes addressed, stamped, and ready to go—*YOU make it all happen.*

Handling the publicity is only a part of the total marketing effort, but it can be a lot more fun and, in many ways, a lot more satisfying. After all, seeing your words, your photos, and your ideas in print can make a lot of work and worry seem very worthwhile. Be confident in yourself and confident in your talents and abilities. When you are confident in your company and its products, the world will, indeed, beat a path to your company's door—and it will be *your* publicity program that told them where to knock.

Newspaper people have a particular way of ending a story or piece of copy that shows it is complete. It looks like this: -30-.

We now bring this chapter to a close.

–30–

6

Direct Mail

Direct mail (or as it is more recently called "Direct Marketing") should not be confused with mail order which, as the name implies, is designed to solicit orders through the mail. Direct mail, as it applies to this dicussion, is usually used to soften up prospects for a follow-up sales call. Many of the ideas included in Chapter 2, Planning and Budgeting, can also help with your direct mail programs.

Please keep in mind as you read this chapter that there are many specialists in this area who can supply lists of prospects, creative capabilities, and the mechanical operations (mailing, sorting, stuffing, etc.) that you may find essential in assembling and distributing a mailing program of any substantial size. This is an area in which many new communicators try to go it alone and often find, to their regret, that most direct mail programs are considerably more complex than they appear on the surface.

The old "shotgun versus rifle shot" analogy really comes alive when you get into direct mail. Not only can you find the companies or people who need your product or services, but you can single them out by state, city, street (right down to which side of the street), name, sex, creed, and title. You can hone in on prospects with such accuracy that it is more than a rifle shot. It is operating with a high-powered rifle with a telescopic lens. And yet, would you believe that many advertising and promotional people who are otherwise rather sophisticated almost completely overlook direct mail? In order to attract prospects, you have to make people aware of your company's products or services. What more direct and economical method is there to promote your company or services than via a mailing to people who qualify as good prospects?

THE SKY IS NOT THE LIMIT

With direct mail advertising, your creativity and ingenuity can soar into outer space. You have an almost limitless array of possibilities when it comes to size, color, and shape. You can make it as large or as small as you want. You can use any kind of paper and any colors of ink you want. You can die-cut it to the shape of your machine or product, emboss it to simulate feel, even perfume it to imitate the aroma (if your product has one). You decide what you hope to achieve and you will be amazed at how swiftly some smart printer, lithographer, or finisher will find a way to accomplish what you have in mind.

MIX AND MATCH

Numerous elements will affect your selection of the physical form of your printed mailing piece. Your first consideration is the purpose for which the direct mail package is designed. Almost all direct mail can be divided into four groups according to purpose:

1. *To inform:*   Direct mail that carries news or information, such as announcements of new products or new models, change in location or phone number, or a change in prices or rates for a product or service.

2. *To persuade:*   Direct mail written primarily for the purpose of persuading or selling.

3. *To remind:*   Direct mail that reminds the recipient of an already established fact.

4. *To instruct:* Direct mail whose main purpose is to impart useful "how to" information or directions.

Most forms of direct mail have a dual or multiple function and fall into more than one group. The group classification can be helpful, however, in clarifying your own thinking as to what you want to accomplish with your mailing.

MORE THAN A FEW

As we said, there are more than a few forms of direct mail. After selecting your format, you are halfway toward selecting the physical form. Some of the more common forms of direct mail are letters, folders, circulars, broadsides, booklets, brochures, self-mailers, postcards, catalogs, programs, invitations, price lists, sales, research and informative bulletins, surveys, calendars, coupons, memorandums, posters, reprints, novelties—you name it! It all goes through the mail!

WHERE TO BEGIN

Begin with answering the same old five W's. (We warned you we would be running into the W's again and again.) Before you write and produce your direct mail piece, you must clearly define what it is to contain and what you expect it to accomplish. The best way to start is by drawing up a strategy sheet and getting the answers to all those time-honored, basic W questions down on paper. Who? What? When? Why? Where? Can you get any more basic?

WHOM DO I WANT TO READ MY MAIL?

Of course, at this stage it is important to know names and addresses. But it is crucial also to have a reader profile. Just who is this Jane or Joe? Are you targeting knowledgeable people or neophytes, old hands or first-time users? Are these people decision makers with purchasing power or decision influences? Are they in a targeted marketing segment or a mixture of industries?

WHAT SHOULD THE MAILING ACCOMPLISH?

There is usually more than one answer to this question. Be sure to list your answers by priority. Are you trying to increase company awareness, reinforce other activities such as PR and advertising, generate sales leads, add new names to your mailing list, introduce a new product or service, or provoke a response for further information, such as a brochure?

WHAT SHOULD THE READER DO?

The person receiving your mail must be given a reason to act and a choice of actions. Are you going to send more detailed information, give a free demonstration, make a sales call, or hold a seminar? Do you want the reader to call or return the enclosed reply card?

WHAT ARE MY COSTS?

Some direct mail includes a gift for the reader. Everyone enjoys getting gifts! Besides, it is a good way to get your mailing past a secretary or other sentry who is screening all incoming mail. However, you must remember that including even a small gift item increases your packaging and postage costs in addition to the price of the gift item and the printing charges.

WHEN SHOULD I MAIL?

This deserves more thought than just picking a date out of the air. For instance, if you are timing the mailing to coincide with a new product or service announcement, plan to mail at least three to five days before the announcement date. If you are telling customers and prospects that this is their last chance to buy before a price increase takes effect, you have to give them plenty of time to buy, which should be at least a few weeks before the price change. Once you determine when the mailing date should be, work your schedule back from there, allowing time for labeling and stuffing envelopes, printing, writing and layout, list selection and purchase, and whatever else goes into your individual mix. You will find that most mailings require six to eight weeks of preparation before the actual mailing date.

WHERE DO I GET THE NAMES?

Begin your list of names with your present customers. They are prime prospects for your current and new products and services. But do not stop there. There are certain to be more prime prospects out there. New customers and prospects are coming into your world all the time. Thumb through telephone books for new listings. Get local business listings from the Chamber of Commerce. Look in your library business directories. Some business directories list the names and titles of company executives and managers. If personnel names are not given, you can always call the company. You will find that you get no flack at all as long as you ask only for a few names at a time. Requesting annual reports from companies and corporations is also a good source. Many publishers will make all or part of their circulation list available to you. And, finally, there are the list brokers. Most of the lists can be broken down by SIC code (Standard Industrial Classification), job title, and ZIP code. Because of these breakdowns, you do not have to go as far and wide as you might otherwise. This is especially good news if your budget is somewhat modest. You can buy a region like New England, one large metropolis like Manhattan, or a few key cities from coast to coast.

HOW MUCH IS ENOUGH?

It is possible to have too much of a good thing. Make sure you make only as many mailings as you can effectively follow up. Otherwise, you can do yourself almost as much harm as good if you appear slow and unresponsive. You want to be able to send the literature, make the sales call, give the demonstration, send the merchandise (or whatever you promised) to all who respond, and do it in a timely fashion.

The following illustrates three "teaser-type" mailings that were followed with an explanatory letter. This particular campaign was used to introduce a new inquiry follow-up system to a company's salespeople and the rep organization. Teaser mailings can be very effective, but they must be handled carefully and creatively (usually with some humor). They are often employed to introduce new products, and their chief purpose is to incite curiosity about the material that will follow. (See Fig. 6–1.)

The following letter was mailed after three "teasers" were sent to a sales force to excite their interest and curiosity. A small plastic doll, "The Troll," was affixed and the meaning of the teasers was explained.

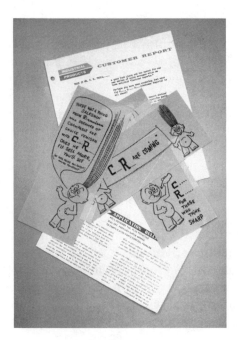

Figure 6–1. Teasers and follow-up letter. (Used with permission of Dennison Manufacturing Company, 275 Wyman St., Waltham, MA 02154.)

Sample: Teaser Follow-Up

Dear (Salesperson's name):

We suppose you have been wondering what all the C. . . R. . . Teaser cards mean. Well, it is all just to get your attention and to prepare you for our new Customer Report product application program. C. . . R. . . stands for Customer Report and, if that is not bad enough, "The Troll" is a little plastic doll that the ad manager swears brings good luck.

But, here is the story. Every week, starting today, we will send you a report similar to the one attached. It will be a case history of a specific product application encountered in the field. Customer Reports will be written for Tags (coded blue), Labels (coded green), Pres-a-ply (coded orange), and Special Products (coded red). We are also sending along a specially prepared, easel-type presentation binder. We ask that, as you receive these reports, you put them in the sections marked by the appropriate color-coded separators. In this way, you will have a growing collection of case histories, filed by individual product line, to show prospects interested in that particular type of application.

Purpose of the Customer Reports

1. To let you know the various applications being sold and the problems being solved in other territories.

2. To provide you with a new sales tool with which you can show a given prospect how we have performed on a given job (perhaps similar to the one the prospect is looking for)—*produce* a sample for him or her to look at—and *spell out* the particular benefits derived by the specific customer mentioned in the report.

The Care and Feeding of Trolls

Trolls are considered lucky! Mr. C. R. Troll (attached) is especially designed to bring luck in sales.

Use these reports as conversation starters, and when your collection of applications has grown, select prospects with applications similar to those spelled out in the reports and watch good fortune—and

purchasing agents will smile on you and yours.
Sincerely,

▶

DIRECT MAIL LIST SOURCES AND APPROACHES

The following is an agency memo that includes six specific recommendations for developing sources for direct mail lists and prospect sources: publications, sales lists, current customers, former customers, prime target market, and rep organizations.

◀ ─────────────────────────────────

Sample: Direct Mail List Sources and Approaches

To: Client
From: Agency
Subject: Suggested Direct Mail Program

   1. The agency suggests that the subscriber list of appropriate publications, especially those currently on our space schedule, be purchased. Since most publications break down their subscribers by title, we recommend that portions of the total list be selected that include only data processing managers and office managers. These are the decision-making authorities who appear most appropriate for your particular division. The agency will prepare a general information direct mail package developed specifically for these individuals, most of whom will have some awareness of the company and its products through previous exposure to our space advertising program.

   2. It is suggested that company salespeople provide a list of their most important prospects. These individuals or companies can then be targeted with a more personal and extensive direct mail effort. The package sent to this audience might include a sample of the product along with copy that might read as follows: "Congratulations! You have been selected to receive the finest quality tape cassette calibration tool available . . ." (final copy will be submitted at a later date).

Since these major prospects have been selected as prime targets, this campaign should not only have special attention and extra budgeting but should also be kept on as a continuing direct mail program with continuing sales follow-up.

3. A special direct mail program should be directed to former customers who once provided lucrative sales and who are still known to be purchasing our type of product. This campaign will be similar to the one above but in this instance, copy might run along the line of: "Remember us? Just in case you have forgotten, we are enclosing a free calibration cassette . . ." (copy will follow once campaign has been approved).

4. A special and continuing direct mail campaign should be designed and directed at present customers. This follows the traditional thinking that our present customer is also our most important prospect. This direct mail program can range in purpose from a simple reminder letter to a "special sale" announcement during a traditionally slow period. Phone orders can also be encouraged through this regular program.

5. An additional mailing program should be targeted to the prime target mail order houses, since this is an excellent outlet for large-scale sales. An effective campaign here will require the mailing of a dozen tapes in a specially designed package, as well as some form of additional inducement (price discount, point-of-sale rack, etc.). This campaign will require extensive follow-up, both by phone and by personal sales visits.

6. Special direct mail programs on a regular basis should be directed to the entire rep organizations. This mailing can be tied to a space advertising campaign and copies of our ads and other promotional materials can be forwarded along to the rep in this mailing. In addition, mailings should be designed to approach established reps in areas where we currently do not have distribution. Last, we suggest that the reps be asked to forward lists of their most important prospects, as well as established customers, in order that we may make mailings from the home office on their behalf. This last program, asking for and using lists from the sales rep, is particularly effective because it accomplishes two ends. First, it pleases the reps and encourages their efforts as it

shows the company is backing them; and second, it provides a current list of known prospects who can be targeted with professional mailing pieces.

Sincerely,

PURPOSES OF DIRECT MAIL

The following checklist delineates some of the varied purposes that direct mail can serve.

1. Encourage, motivate, and provide materials and information to salespeople to improve sales. Show new customers that they are appreciated.

2. Pre-inform your marketing and advertising programs to your channels of distribution.

3. Develop a database of prospect mailing lists.

4. Announce new product lines and new reps or dealers.

5. Inform customers of special sales and other inducements to have them come to your retail outlet.

6. Establish a demand for your products.

7. Let customers know you are thinking of them even when you are not calling on a regular basis.

8. Open the door for sales calls.

9. Define special groups and talk to them on their own terms.

10. Keep in touch with customers not currently buying.

11. Approach the financial community, including shareholders in your company.

12. Provide an educational program to inform your reps of the technical details of your product.

13. Motivate prospects after the salesperson has made a call.

14. Follow-up on inquiries received from publication advertising.

15. Provide an abundance of new prospects from inquiries received through your mailing programs.

HOW TO WRITE AN EFFECTIVE DIRECT MAIL LETTER

The art of writing an effective direct mail letter is so critical and somewhat unique that we must give it special emphasis here even at the risk of being somewhat redundant.

The first requirement in producing an effective direct mail letter is that it must be organized in outline form with special effort being made to talk directly to the intended reader. In addition, a direct mail letter should center on one basic idea. This central idea should be the core issue and everything that does not contribute to this central theme should be thrown out. Once you have established your central idea, organize everything else around it.

The AIDCA (Attention, Interest, Desire, Conviction, Action) formula, which we go into in greater detail in Chapter 10, is an excellent starting point for almost any direct mail letter you will write. If you follow this method, your letter will get the reader's attention and interest, influence his or her thinking, and obtain action. Remember, throughout your writing effort keep the central idea constantly in mind; organize your message according to the above formula, and you will never write pointless rambling letters. It is also important to remember that you can use small words to express large ideas. Lincoln's Gettysburg Address effectively illustrates this concept. Considered to be one of the greatest works ever written, it has only 265 words and contains 197 one-syllable words (74.3 percent), 48 two-syllable words (18.1 percent), 13 three-syllable words (5 percent), and only 7 four-syllable words (2.6 percent).

It will serve you well to get a hold of some of the books we have already mentioned on writing and it will benefit you to pick up some material specifically involved with direct mail copy as well. Direct mail requires a special kind of writing that demands that you write simply, naturally, and interestingly so that your reader will get your point quickly. Use the following checklist as a guide for writing copy for direct mail.

1. Did you get your reader involved with your opening sentence?

2. Is the lead sentence too long? Does it make the central point?

3. Do you include the benefit to the reader in your opening lines?

4. Do you have your biggest benefits at the top?

5. Are your thoughts arranged in an orderly succession?

6. Is your copy completely believable?

7. Have you asked the reader to respond or have you requested that the reader take some action?

8. Do you have a reply letter or envelope that ties in with the overall package? (See Fig. 6–2.)

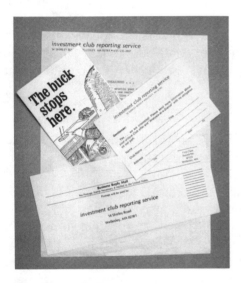

Figure 6–2. Sample direct mail package including: cover letter, brochure, response card, and return envelope.

TESTING YOUR DIRECT MAIL PROGRAMS

Volumes have been written on how to test direct mail operations scientifically, especially list effectiveness. Rather than go into the heavy statistical analysis kind of testing that large-volume mailing houses need to conduct, we have outlined a simpler, trial-and-error approach that will serve the purpose of testing regular-sized direct mail packages.

A trial-and-error method will not give you the kind of full results you would get from a total testing program, however, it will provide some information upon which you can make your mailing programs more effective.

There are many kinds of direct mail testing methods, but for our purposes we will consider only those we have termed the "single-package test." In our package test, the trick is to find out from a single sample what you can expect from your entire mailing. The sample is designed to tell you how many customers may be contained on a particular list and how many sales might be available from that list. Simply stated, you draw one sample and from that sample you analyze the effectiveness of your entire program. The catch, of course, is that you will want to vary the package and test the various components it may contain. In the listing below, we have indicated some of the variations you may test in a given "package mailing." It is most important that you test only one variable at a time.

Type of offer	Typography of enclosure
Type of postage used	Format of enclosure
Size of outgoing envelope	Copy used for order blank
Appearance of package	Art of order blank
Copy used in sales letter	Format of order blank
Art in sales letter	Type of return postage
Format of sales letter	Format of return envelope
Typography of sales letter	Time of mailing
Type of enclosure	Time of arrival
Art of enclosure	

If each of the above factors (and there are, of course, many others) had only two choices (for example, first-class mail versus third-class; no return postage versus return paid; postal card or short letter versus long letter; plain envelope versus illustrated envelope; rational copy versus emotional copy; black-and-white versus color printing; etc.) you can see that there are almost a limitless number of different combinations that you could check. And there are more choices as you go deeper. For instance, the same piece of copy can be printed in 100 typefaces. The same piece of art can be used in dozens of ways. The same layout can be printed in different colors and on various kinds of paper stock. There is practically no end to the elements you can vary.

But whatever you do when testing, *test one variable, and only one, at a time!*

Here is a checklist which will keep you on the beam. Ask yourself these questions:

1. What is it specifically I wish to test?

2. How can I manipulate my material so that the thing I wish to test will be the one and only variable?

3. Can I keep everything else constant except the single variable that is the substance of the test?

4. What is the smallest sample I must take, considering the percentage of error I can accept.

5. What is the simplest methodology for the test?

6. Is the test constructed so that I can tabulate and analyze results quickly and simply?

ANALYZING RESULTS

There is a range of statistical methods that will set up direct mail tests and analyze results. It is often wise to take your mailing to experts in this field, especially if it is complex or if you are just starting to develop your programs. This is because you are sure to have some bias in your own program, and your ideas can change even as the test is being conducted.

DETERMINING CONCLUSIONS FROM TEST RESULTS

When it is all over and your test results are tabulated, you will find that conclusions fall into three categories:

1. Conclusions you already suspected.

2. Conclusions that confirm or refute your hunches about a given mailing list, mailing piece, or mailing method.

3. Conclusions you never thought of before and, in some cases, you may even have difficulties believing. When that happens, *believe in your tests.*

RETAIL DIRECT MAIL SPECIAL

Although we have tried not to separate industrial, technical, and consumer programs as a general rule, in the case of direct mail programs there are special considerations that we believe retailers especially should be aware of and make a part of their internal operations.

If you have a retailing operation, you may wish to do the following:

1. Set up an easy system for recording the name of every person who *enters* your store. Place these names on a prospect list.

2. Record the name of every person who *buys* in your store. Set these names up on a special buyers list for frequent promotion.

3. Get information about anniversaries, weddings, births, and similar special occasions for both buyers and prospects. Set up an automatic system for mailing greeting cards to your customers and prospects for these occasions. They will appreciate it.

4. Design low-cost promotional pieces for use as "envelope stuffers" with every invoice you send out. Do this every month in the year, featuring seasonal items.

5. Define the consumer market radius from which you draw business then set up a mailing list covering all residences in this prime consumer area.

6. Establish a regular mailing schedule for reaching:
   a. Your general neighborhood prospect list
   b. Your charge account customer list
   c. Your buyer list
   d. Your store visitor list.

7. Notify all segments of your list of "advance private sales" and other special events whenever possible. This applies particularly to your charge account list and your buyers list.

8. Begin to prepare a Christmas catalog not later than June 1 for mailing immediately after Labor Day.

9. Give your customers and prospective buyers every possible opportunity to buy from you by mail—encourage mail order business.

POST-PAID REPLY VEHICLES

Business reply mail is a service provided by the United States Post Office for which it charges postage on only the mail that is returned from your original mailing (business reply cards, for example). We suggest that you go in person to your local post office and establish a rapport with your local postmaster. The post office is a most important resource and can provide help with postal activities in areas other than reply mail. The post office will apprise you of the current regulations for obtaining permit applications and bring you up to date on fees and prepayment regulations and other requirements including special formats. And, of course, the post office will update you on postal costs and increases.

BULK MAILING

A direct mailing program of any substantial size (over 200) should be mailed under the bulk mailing rate discount by the post office. Again, you should check with your local postmaster for an update on requirements for bulk rate such as fee, permit, minimum number of pieces, ZIP coding, bundling, facing, prepayment specifications, and the like. Remember that although bulk mailing provides certain cost-saving advantages, it is sometimes preferable to send your mailing first class, provided that it does not fall into the circular or "junk" mail category.

PROGRAM CHECKLIST FOR EFFECTIVE DIRECT MAIL

In summary, we present yet another recap of checkpoints that have proven to be important contributors to all types and sizes of direct mail programs. Before launching into this area, answer the following:

1. What are you trying to accomplish?

      This is probably the single most important decision you will make concerning your direct mail and it is one that many communicators neglect.
   a. Do you want mass inquiries to select from or do you want high-potential, qualified sales leads?
   b. Are you after overall sales increases or do you want sales with higher margins which are more profitable?
   c. Do you want leads that you will need to convert or do you want an immediate sales result from your initial inquiries?

      These are the kind of questions you must ask yourself before you even attempt to put your program together. The objective that you decide on will dictate the type, cost, and the entire direction of your mailing.

2. Do you have the right mailing list?
   a. Do you have a profile on the prospects you are trying to reach?
   b. Does the list you have acquired direct itself to this profile?
   c. Have you evaluated the mailing lists available from brokers as opposed to your own in-house list?
   d. Have you looked at the number of undelivered returns (sometimes referred to as "nixies")?
   e. Have you checked the results from addressing to titles rather than personal names?

3. Did you write benefit copy?
   Review the material above covering direct mail copy.
   a. Have you pictured the benefit in the headline?
   b. Have you told the readers specifically what they can expect and have you backed up all claims with proof and testimonials?
   c. Have you informed the readers of what they might lose if they do not act, repeated your most important benefits, and asked for action in your close?

4. Did you dress up your mailing to suit your audience?

    a. Have you kept your mailing in the same tone as the market you are attempting to reach?

    b. Does your mailing match your audience? (You would choose a different approach for business secretaries than for medical technicians.)

Your direct mail package will be quite different when presenting a big-ticket item when compared to a low-cost advertising specialty. Your copy can be more whimsical when announcing a sale close-out than it will be when making a serious fund-raising effort. It is extremely important to match your direct mail package to the audience at which it is directed.

5. Have you made it easy for your prospects to respond?

    a. Does your mailing include devices to incite the prospect to action such as free information, pre-trial offer, free gift, and money-back guarantees?

Remember, it is most important that you provide a pre-addressed, postage-paid reply envelope or card.

6. Do you have a regular direct mail program?

It is interesting to note that very few salespeople expect to close a sale the first time they approach a prospect. Yet many companies do not have a continuing program of repeat mailings. It is important to have a consistent campaign with regular mailings released frequently throughout the year.

7. Are you continuing to test your mailings?

The only way you can improve on your direct mail results is to test and revise constantly. And you might ask yourself, should this testing also include your products and services as well as your mailings?

7

Space Advertising

Perhaps more time, energy, and money is devoted to the area of mass-media publication advertising than any other promotional area. The total company image as well as product acceptability and usefulness are laid on the line before the entire target market with a space ad. Space or publication advertising encompasses ads that are printed in designated spaces provided by publications for distribution to subscribers. This type of advertising has become increasingly important as the cost of personal sales calls has risen astronomically. Results of space advertising can be measured not only in increased sales but also in the improved prestige and acceptance of the entire company, including its products and services.

ADVERTISING FOR ALL

Space advertising is not magic and it cannot work miracles, but it absolutely, positively makes sense to utilize publication advertising. People who don't believe in advertising are more than behind the times. They're living in the Dark Ages. And before long, that lack of vision will be reflected in their business—or, more appropriately, in the lack thereof.

SIZE IS NO CRITERION

Space advertising is not only for the rich and prosperous. All companies and services can benefit from this type of advertising. And, oftentimes, the smaller you are, the more the need exists and the bigger the benefit.

THE HUMBLE POSTCARD

Once upon a time, long before Frank Perdue began to fluff up his feathers and fly, a man who delivered fresh eggs, chickens, and turkeys house to house used postal cards to announce his arrival in new territories. It helped him build a profitable business that extended over half a state. And, as everyone knows, you can hardly get a less expensive medium than the humble postal card. Perhaps you're saying to yourself, "Home delivery! You must be the ghost of Christmas Past and talking about the Good Old Days. Postcards couldn't possibly work today, could they?" And we answer, "You bet!" Not only can they be one of the most inexpensive, cost-effective, and efficient means of "announcement" advertising but they are an excellent means of "reminder" advertising as well. A great deal of product and service sales can be and are prompted by just such a simple device as a postal card.

A SIMPLE MESSAGE

All the card has to say is "You last (bought or did something) on such a date. Isn't it time that you thought about (buying or doing it) again?" The product can be any disposable item in the world. Supplies of any sort are naturals and the same can be said of most services—whether it is having your teeth cleaned, your eyes checked, or your car's oil changed.

POSTCARDS AND SPACE ADVERTISING

But isn't this chapter about space advertising? What's with postcards? Well, first of all, many magazine publishers make postcard pack mailing available to their circulations. Called "card-deck" mailings, this type of direct mail is extremely effective and usually produces considerably more inquiries than a space ad in the same publication. However, the point we wish to make is about your own direct mail programs. As inexpensive an advertising medium as postcards are, even they don't make sense all the time. Often, even a most modest budget invested in space advertising makes a lot more sense. (See Fig. 7-1.)

IT'S SIMPLE ARITHMETIC

Let's say that it makes sense to advertise your product or service in a national publication reaching 600,000 readers. We'll put a reasonably high price on your small space ad, which may be in one of those "Shoppers' Guide" or classified advertising sections—about $1,000 an insertion. You decide that you want to go for the "whole nine yards,"

Figure 7-1. Publication postal "packs." (Used with permission of *Office Magazine,* 1600 Summer St., Stamford, CT 06912.)

which, in this instance, is twelve times (twelve insertions a year). Your space ad cost of $12,000 reaches 600,000 readers every month for a full year. If, on the other hand, you were to mail postal cards to 600,000 homes or businesses *just once, at today's postage rate,* ($.15 each for first-class postcard) it would cost you a whopping $90,000 (600,000 × $.15) for first-class postage to this same number of prospects. A significant difference, wouldn't you agree? (Yes, we know that postage would be considerably less if mailed bulk and/or other discounted postal rates. Nonetheless, direct mail to this number would be astronomically higher than going with a space ad in a publication with this circulation.) The point is that, as useful and inexpensive certain media are (such as the postcard), they become uneconomical if used beyond certain limits.

MIRACLES AND MYTHS

Let's put one myth to rest before we continue. Some people think advertising can sell inferior products and services. It simply is not so, never has been, and never will be. Advertising cannot make silk purses out of sows' ears. In fact, just the opposite is true. Advertising can sell value, but it cannot make up for the lack of it. It cannot win continued preference for inferior products or services. What advertising *will* do is force the inferior product or service out of the market faster than if it were not advertised. Indeed, it has been said that the best advertisement is a good product and the best promotion is word of mouth.

However, given a good product or service, such as yours, advertising can carry it to new heights of public esteem, usage, sales volume, and profit. This is absolutely true whether your business is big or small (and whether or not your budget matches your size).

A BASIC SELLING IDEA

You've heard it before and you're going to hear it again: The continuous sale of a product by advertising calls for a central theme—a basic idea or a general strategy around which all of the advertising can be built! (Refer to "Unique Selling Propositions" in Chapter 1 and the material on "Basic Themes" discussed in writing the brochure in Chapter 4.)

It is axiomatic in advertising that your reader and prospect will remember a single forceful claim and only one concept. Check any ad campaign you consider especially effective and memorable, and invariably you will be able to discern a basic selling idea or message, whether it's labeling Lipton Tea as "brisk," Wendy's much attention-getting "Where's the beef?," or Michelin Tires' "Because you've got so much riding on them."

WHAT DO YOU KNOW?

If, right from the start, you know what your basic selling idea is, wonderful! You are far luckier than most of the world's advertising copywriters. Embryo authors are told over and over again, "Write about what you know; don't attempt to write about something you don't know." This is all well and good for authors. Copywriters, on the other hand, are continually called upon to write about things about which, at the outset, they know very little or nothing at all. Still, they're expected to be brilliant and to the point, discovering and stressing a basic selling idea, a unique selling proposition, or a theme. And, that is precisely what many do. You can, too! But if you start out at ground zero, as most of us do, it takes some real digging.

WHERE DOES THE DIGGING BEGIN?

The kind of information you require, and hopefully will acquire, is, of course, influenced by the type of product or service you are promoting. Certainly, not all of the paths that we suggest exploring may be appropriate for you to follow, but the principle they illustrate is.

The important thing, whatever your product or service, is to explore every avenue, turn over every stone, and check out the light at the end of every tunnel. Know more about your product than you ever expected to know. Know more than you think you'll ever need to know. Then you're ready to really write about it with understanding and conviction.

DISPELLING ANOTHER MYTH

One persistent myth, even among people who should know better, is that successful advertising writers sit around waiting for a muse to perch on their shoulders and whisper impelling phrases in their ears. The reality is far less romantic. Blood, sweat, and tears are more like the true scenario. So, don't be discouraged if you find yourself having to "work things out" rather than "whip them out." Believe us, you're in the best of company. Nowhere more than in writing ads does the "ten percent inspiration and ninety percent perspiration" cliché apply.

THE PRELUDE BEGINS

Take the product you are about to promote into your mind's eye and turn it over and over, exploring every facet. Some solid gold (in the form of a real gem of an idea) may be hidden in a crevice. Therefore, carefully examine all the following facets of your product.

1. What is it made of? The raw materials that go into a product can sometimes be very important for you to know about. Northern Tissue was promoted successfully for many years on the idea that it was "softer because it is made of fluff." This was a direct result of the copywriter's exposure to a paper mill. Charmin built a notable TV campaign around its own version of incredible (or credible, if you will) softness. And, as for coffee, maybe "mountain grown" really does make happier and heartier beans, as Folger's would like us to believe.

The "raw materials" of service are personnel, abilities, facilities, and convenience. "We'll respond to your call, no matter what the hour, be it day or night" is certainly a great theme for just about any service imaginable. You'll find the right theme will come to mind if you just keep searching.

2. How well is it made? Even if your product is made of the same basic materials as your competitors use, there can be a significant difference in the finished item due to extra steps, expertise, or care in the making. In the area of service, "People make the difference" is a fabulous theme for a professional group (and one that we have used more than once for different clients with different markets).

3. What does it do? Some products satisfy more than a single desire. Some are quite singular in their function. The same may be said about services. If you have a product or service with a well-defined function, it is better not to stray too far from that fact when you develop your theme. If you are pushing fountain pens, for instance, material, design, color, and product recognition may all play a part in your promotion. You might even have a nice product difference in that your pen may hold more ink than competitive pens. But the function of pens is to write. Along with any additional appeals you stress, you had best establish the fact that your pen writes well. If you are selling anti-static carpeting to the high-tech community for use in labs and offices where static-sensitive computers, control, and test equipment is operating, you may want to lay some stress on beauty and comfort (a prime appeal of consumer carpeting). However, you must not lose sight of the fact that an imperative, from the user's point of view, is the carpet's static control capability.

4. How well does it do it? A primary objective of most, if not all, advertising is to establish the fact that the advertiser's product offers greater operating advantages or user satisfaction than what is available from other sources. If your product is the absolute and unqualified best in its field, you should have no trouble getting this conviction into your copy. The fact of life is that there are many good products and services, but few unqualified bests. Usually it is a trade-off. Your product is better than that of your competition in some way or ways, and weaker in others. Your job is to convince the buyer that, whatever your product or service is best in is, indeed, the most important aspect of that product or service.

It is not a bad idea to begin with the realization that nobody is interested in your product per se. This tried-and-true axiom cannot be overemphasized. To understand it is the beginning of advertising wisdom. To work with it always in mind is the first step toward successful advertising. Although value is really intrinsic, it usually lies in the eyes and mind of the beholder. As one leading advertising light has said,

"Don't tell people how good you make your goods, tell them how good your goods make them."

Users of a product are not really interested in the product itself but in what that product will do for them. Thus, the surest way to engage the readers' or potential users' attention and concern is to present the product in terms of their interest. First of all, you should begin to think about the effect or influence the product may have on the life of the person who buys it. An able and established writer comes up with such effects and influences seemingly by intuition, but actually that intuition is sound judgment aided by long experience.

If you are a beginner, you are advised to make a checklist. One of the shortest courses in the evaluation of current effective advertising approaches is to study the ads in magazines and newspapers in your field and spend a few evenings with the commercials on radio and television. This should enable you to make a comprehensive list of some of the current basic selling appeals and to observe the various ways in which these appeals are presented. In composing a checklist, it is advisable to write the various selling approaches in the form of questions. A good checklist would certainly contain the following questions, and you should answer them in relation to your product as far as possible:

1. Will the product make the user feel more important and how?

Just about everyone wants to be more important, and this is a powerful selling appeal provided you can make it stick. Your readers unquestionably want to be more important and they have to be convinced that your product or service will make them so. In using this appeal, you should get into the ad as much support as possible for your claim. If you can't really support your claim, you had best investigate one that you can. General Motors uses the "feel more important appeal" very skillfully and successfully in its advertising for Cadillac cars. The copy is sometimes long, interesting, and, almost always, beautifully written, but, it essentially says, "Few other possessions will proclaim your position and importance in the world as well as a Cadillac!" In reality, the cost of the car and the character of the car support the claim, thus making it believable. Johnnie Walker whiskey bases its appeal on the same "you are important" approach. The implication of such advertising is that the purchase of the product identifies the buyer as a connoisseur or makes the buyer a connoisseur; because Johnnie Walker is a good Scotch, expensive and important, imported and famous, the choice is creditable. IBM did essentially the same thing with the introduction of its computers. Customers felt that they were getting the very best and that if their company had IBM equipment, it was a big important company. The buyers felt secure in the belief that they had bought the best and were not in a position to be criticized.

2. Will the product make the buyer happier and, if so, why?

Happiness is also a universal desire, but it is not enough merely to make the claim that the product will make the user happier. The claim should be supported with convincing reasons why. The Cunard Shipping Company used the "it will make you happier" theme well with its slogan, "Getting there is half the fun!" The copy always went on to extol delicious food, luxurious accommodations, relaxing atmosphere, and congenial companionship, all of which pays off in making your travel more fun. Computer advertisers use the same tact with their user-friendly approaches and the fact that you will be able to do your work faster and easier on menu-driven equipment.

3. Will the product make the purchaser more comfortable and, if so, when?

This is an appeal that creeps into the advertising for a wide variety of products and services. It is used widely, of course, for clothing and furniture, and can also apply to air conditioning, lighting, and all sorts of things that are used in almost every environment.

4. Will the product make the user more prosperous and how?

If one excludes hobos, philosophers, and bag ladies, the desire for greater income and prosperity is virtually universal. There are two ways in which a product or service can promise increased prosperity to the user. One is by increasing the user's income; the other is by reducing the user's expenses. In its advertising to enroll students for home-study courses, international correspondence schools have a long and successful history of promising increased income and making good on the promise. Typically, in one advertisement they express higher income in such mouth-watering terms as they speak of the salary increase as "the kind your boss asks you not to talk about."

United Air Lines follows the same tact when it shows two gentlemen in a high-flying plane with the story line that they left Los Angeles an hour ago and will be in Philadelphia a few hours later and that they know they are saving valuable time.

5. Will the product make work easier for the purchaser and how much easier?

Some wit once remarked that labor-saving devices were more than likely invented by lazy people. The desire to have one's work made easier is also quite universal. No one will question that a vacuum cleaner is easier to use than a broom, but it is harder to demonstrate that one certain vacuum cleaner makes work much easier than another.

6. Will the product give the purchaser greater security and how?

Security is another universal desire. Four distinct areas with which advertising is most often concerned are: (1) security for the individual, which has certainly become a far more critical one in world affairs, especially for top executives, diplomats, and all sorts of individuals; (2) security for the family; (3) security for the home; and (4) security for the business.

This last security for the business could include advertising for an office safe, which would put the security of a business first, and perhaps talk about how your business security rests in the protection of your records. Copy says such things as, "Do you have the notion that your fire insurance will cover all your losses? You will find out that you will have to prepare a proof-of-loss statement before you can collect fully." It points out that many other brands of safes turn out to be incinerators in a fire, turning supposedly safe records to ashes.

Greater security is an effective advertising theme provided it is in character with the product or service that is advertised.

7. Will the product make the purchaser more attractive or better liked, and how?

This appeal is often on thinner ice than several of the others. It is used in all sorts of cosmetics and clothing advertising, and it should be approached with caution unless you can really support it with your product facts. The classic example, of course, is the theme used in the advertising of Dale Carnegie's book, *How to Win Friends and Influence People.* The book was an all-time best-seller. People had confidence in the advertising and they had confidence in Dale Carnegie. They believed that he could give them advice that would help them. This yearning to be attractive, to be liked, and to be popular provides you with an important emotional appeal. This approach works most effectively today as witnessed by the approaches used in promoting the plethora of self-help books.

8. Will the product give the user some distinction?

A desire to stand out from the crowd a little or a lot is also a very strong and universal one. In the service area, this is the reason some industries pay large sums of money to a publicity agent to keep their names and photographs constantly in the press. It is the very same human desire that causes people to have initials engraved on cuff links or cut into the shutters on their house. It sells monograms on towels and on matchbooks, and it also inspires people to collect everything from bird feathers to turn-of-the-century automobiles. In varying degrees, many kinds of products can confer some distinction upon the user; all you have to do is dig a little deeper to find in what way your product or service will do so.

9. Will the product improve, protect, or maintain the health of the purchaser now?

With very few exceptions, health is a common concern in all times, for all sorts of people. If your product or service makes a genuine contribution to the maintenance, protection, or improvement of health, this fact can be a very persuasive one to include in your advertising or even to make your major selling theme. Of course, the appeal in this area is very obvious for all types of off-the-shelf medical and preventive medicines. Bayer aspirin is probably one of the most widely used and understood of these. It is used to relieve headaches and all kinds of pains; it is offered as a gargle for your throat; it is taken at the beginning of a cold; and, most recently, it is used as a preventive of heart attacks. In addition, this "protect your health" theme can apply to such items as lighting, clean air devices for factory and office workers, and things under foot to keep people from slipping or falling.

10. Will the product appeal to the purchaser as a bargain?

Almost everyone on earth is looking for a bargain. Some products have, or can be given, a bargain appeal. For example, millions of consumers wait months for "white sales"—when sheets and towels are reduced to a low price by the department stores.

In the selling strategy of Book-of-the-Month Club, advertising was based on the wide popularity of bargains. Theirs is a continuous bargain offer. It is not made to gain a temporary advantage over competition—it comes out of the sales policy of the company. Such an ad is a bid for new members, and as a reward for joining the club, prospective members are always offered an unusually attractive book or books for practically nothing and must agree only to purchase a minimum number of books during the next year or two. Members are told that after fulfilling this obligation they will be given one book for every three buys and can discontinue membership at any time whatever. The selections are always offered at a lower price than what one pays in a book store. It's a bargain from one end to the other.

The bargain appeal can be applied to a range of products, both consumer and industrial, as well as to a variety of services. Oftentimes the bargain can be couched in the terms of "turning in your old equipment and getting the new equipment at a discount."

There are, of course, many other kinds of appeals as well as countless variations on the ones suggested here. But you get the idea; just don't forget to make the appeal fit your product and its audience.

BUILDING THE AD

There are seven essential steps in advertising planning and preparation. Advertising copy, as we are using the term, refers to the entire written portion of the ad—the body copy and the headline. The body copy is all the copy that is set in solid type, that is, everything except the headline. As soon as you know the size, shape, and purpose of your ad and the medium in which it will appear, your path will essentially follow the seven following guideposts:

1. Gather needed facts about the product and service and its use.

2. Arrange a selling outline that includes a sequence of steps for developing the theme and copy platform.

3. Determine your approach and the appeal and use of your strongest interest-rousing factors.

4. Visualize the completed ad in the rough layout form.

5. Write the copy—the body copy and the headlines.

6. Plan the illustration material to support and complement the copy.

7. Prepare the finished layout.

Let's cover a few more basics before we get into our actual process. Here are devices that can turn product interest into buying interest and actually induce product purchases. Some are particularly applicable to specific forms of advertising, such as retail and mail order; others are generally applicable. First you create the desire; next you add conviction; and then you follow with a request for action.

WAYS OF CREATING DESIRE

1. Amplify the promise of your headline if a benefit headline is used.

2. Present other direct benefits.

3. Picture use or ease of operation.

4. Show negatives of troubles avoided by the products purchased.

5. Use beauty, prestige, and social approval angles.

6. Emphasize exclusive advantages and points of superiority.

WAYS OF CONVINCING

1. Emphasize specific selling points that support important benefits.

2. Present evidence and proof based on performance of tests.

3. Use genuine testimonials and endorsements by qualified individuals.

4. Give factual evidence of the product's leadership or popularity.

5. Use guarantees when practical.

6. Build confidence by writing believably and sticking to facts.

WAYS OF INDUCING ACTION

1. Ask the reader to write for a book or sample.

2. A "send coupon" is used both to increase inquiries and to obtain actual orders, as in mail order advertising. (Coupons increase space ad response by as much as 10 to 15 percent, about the same as we discussed in Chapter 6, direct mail.)

3. Set a time limit on your offer or price (a common retail action) such as "a special for this day only" or "this month only" or "this week only."

4. Limit the quantity available.

5. Make a free offer. (Caution: There may be specific legal limitations.)

6. Try suggesting a choice—not a choice of "if" but of "which" you
want.

7. Include installment of credit terms and trade-in allowances.

8. Stress the ease of buying, such as mail, telephone orders, 800 number, free deliveries, and the like.

9. Extend an invitation to your exhibit or sales demonstration.

WORDS, WORDS, WORDS

To really possess power, words must be joined to ideas. A piece of copy
may be polished to the last degree, but it will be without power if it is
not pregnant with meaning. Words can shout, whisper, glisten, or
gleam; they may strut or stride; or they may tumble or collapse. Words
may be odoriferous or fragrant, dull or keen, honest or sly. They may
be lively or slow, vague or clear. In the words themselves, there is a
magic or suggestion. The words *stride* or *strut* are far more concrete
and figurative than the word *walk*. In a similar manner, to *tumble* or
collapse suggests more specific meanings than to *fall*. People can be
moved from the associated effect of pleasant or unpleasant sounds that
are common to large groups of words. For example, most of the *gr*
verbs have unpleasant associations (grunt, groan, growl, gripe, grind).
In contrast, many of the *gl* words have pleasant sound associations
both as verbs and adjectives (glad, glorious, glamorous, gleam, glow,
glisten, glitter).

WORDS TO AVOID

Positively speaking, then, the words that we select should be correct,
commonly understood, and as meaningful as possible either in a literal
or a suggestive way. You are mainly concerned with the positive aspects
of the word you select, so you must be on guard against the use of

words that are wrong for reasons of sound suggestion, poor taste, or obsolescence. Within your own lifetime, certain slang phrases have become obsolete; and within a generation or two, perfectly good words can change meaning or lose their effectiveness. Some words are provincial in use and should be avoided for that reason.

Words that you might want to avoid in your advertising copy could include the following:

1. Words with obviously unpleasant sound associations are less than useful in producing the outcome you hope to create. Pleasant sounds are always more inviting. For instance, with a more pleasing name, perhaps that delightful breakfast food called *grits* might be more popular nationally.

2. Avoid slang of all kinds unless it is particularly apt and currently widespread in use. At various times in the last forty years or more, terms like *skidoo* and *vamoose* meant the same thing that came to be expressed as *scram,* which now is dated. During World War II, *snafu* was an "in" word, probably the successor of *all fouled up.* Today, *hassle* still has some currency, but they are all on the way out.

3. Obsolete words, and those that are fast becoming obsolete, should also be avoided. For example, you know that a *storm* hasn't been a *tempest* since the times of Shakespeare.

4. Provincialisms (regional colloquialisms) should be carefully avoided except in areas where they will be well understood. In New England, people still "pick up a room" whereas in the Pennsylvania Dutch country, they "right it up." In some areas, "leave us do that" is acceptable. Obviously, if your copy is for national issue, you should avoid all provincial expressions.

5. Avoid words that are understood clearly by only a small fraction of the population. Of course, with certain forms of class appeal or in specific audience, the unusual word may be very effective. But if your copy is written for the public in general, you should use words that are understood generally. Of course, sometimes uncommon words move from their uncommonness into commonality. Nowadays everything in the computer world, especially in the software aspects of it, *enhances* things continually; years ago, *enhanced* was a rather uncommon word. Not so long ago, a prominent New York retail store, using an elaborately hand-lettered

headline for a furniture advertisement, had the headline, "Enhance your living room." *Enhance* means to build up or increase, but the copywriter apparently thought it meant to beautify.

6. Do not use words in poor taste. *New Yorker Magazine,* in its humorous fashion, recorded a penciled sign taped to the door of a New York television studio at Madison Square Garden during the Westminster Kennel Club Show. The sign read, "Please do not use the word *bitch* when speaking of female dogs." Here was a case of a word that was in perfectly good usage on the floor of the Kennel Club Show itself and in dog breeding circles everywhere, yet, for reasons of good taste, the word *bitch* was unsuitable for broadcasting.

7. Do not use words that are superfluous. Research shows that twenty-five little words (such as *the, and, that, to, of,* and *for*) account for one-third of all English writing. *The* alone accounts for 5 percent; *and* accounts for 3 percent. Superfluous words add almost nothing to your message or impact.

So we see that words can brighten emphasis and add color or motion, and the use of such words can help sell your product. You must forever check your choice of words, asking yourself: Is the word correct? Is it in good usage? Wherever my message will be read, is it easily understood? Does it carry the right connotation? Is it pleasing in sound? Is it the exact word for my purpose? Is it essential or superfluous?

Visual nouns, lively verb forms, and highly descriptive adjectives create imagery in our advertising copy. Verbs are the liveliest and most colorful of all word forms. Properly used, they will descriptively add motion, action, color, and emphasis. Active verbs move the copy forward; passive verbs or words slow it down!

HEADLINES

Essentially, headlines can be direct or indirect. The direct headline is double-barreled. Ideally, it gives information and makes readers want more information. If it fails to induce readers to read further, it at least leaves them with some persuasive sales point that can make them favorably inclined to the product; thus, the advertiser has some value in such an ad but not necessarily full value.

The indirect headline has complete singleness of purpose. It relies on its ability to make people read the body copy. If it fails, the advertiser has less value than one with a direct headline and sometimes no value at all.

Among the most popular and, in fact, the most effective type of headline you can use is the news headline. That being said, you must remember that few, if any, statements about advertising are universally true. They may apply in a majority of instances, but never without exception. Almost any rule can be disproved by an unusual example.

By and large, however, the news headline is the most effective of all. This is understandable because news is universally interesting. People like to know what is going on; they like to keep up to date; they like to be well informed. The most important requisite of the news headline is that it be news. Because of the popularity, readability, and effectiveness, some writers try to give the impression of news where none exists. Mistakenly, they write such headlines as, "Big news for mothers!" "There is great news for car owners!" "Important news for you!" Later, the writers wonder why their body text didn't get high readership. The answer is obvious. People are neither attracted nor intrigued entirely by the word *news*. They are interested in the news itself. Genuine news does not have to be labeled *news* nor should it be. No headline of genuine news interest needs the word *news* in it.

What is genuine news? The front page of any newspaper can answer that for you. News is anything of widespread interest, whether local or national, about which most people are, as yet, unfamiliar. News is information that has not grown stale. News is self-explanatory. It is difficult to imagine the headlines of a better newspaper reaching the streets exclaiming, "Hot news in Brooklyn!" or "Big news from Washington!" instead of "Fire destroys Brooklyn landmark!" or "Supreme Court justice impeached!" The big difference between newspaper news and advertising news is that advertising news does not have to be so current. Any sales point or benefit to be derived from the product or service is news if the public is unfamiliar with it. Many sales stories have lain dormant for years until some enterprising advertising agent uncovered them, brought them to light, and made them useful and provocative advertising news.

ADVERTISING COPY LENGTH

Copy length has been one of the most common conversation pieces in the advertising world for years. Advertising copy should be long enough to accomplish its objective. This common generalization is sound but hardly specific enough to be helpful. It was reported that Abraham Lincoln was asked how long a speech should be. He responded, "A speech is like a person's legs; the legs should be long enough to reach the ground." The rational course in advertising is to use enough words and enough space to express effective salesmanship for the article advertised. A good ad should be just long enough to accomplish its selling purpose—to produce interest, conviction, and an active buying impulse.

Generally speaking, building primary demand for a product calls for more copy than cultivating the favorable attitude toward an existing brand. It may take long, detailed, and descriptive copy to create consciousness of a new need or to arouse a new desire. Keeping present customers satisfied with a brand, or even getting some to switch from competitive brands, is likely to take less copy.

When your copy is charged with evoking a direct action, such as placing an order, it must perform the complete selling task. Besides attracting attention to the ad and arousing initial interest, you must sustain the interest of the readers. You must convince them that the product is good and should be purchased immediately. To do all these things requires many more words of copy than if you simply wanted to induce a kind of indirect response such as a general feeling on the part of readers that they might try the advertised product at some future time.

WHEN TO USE LONG COPY

In certain situations, long (or relatively long) copy is far more appropriate than brief copy. Here are a number of cases in which copy of considerable length should be seriously considered:

1. The ad is for an industrial product.

2. The ad pertains to specialty goods.

3. The ad is technical or mechanical.

4. The product is new and the market needs to be educated regarding its benefits and characteristics.

5. The ad pertains to a brand that is highly differentiated.

6. The product is high priced.

7. The objective of the ad is to build primary demand.

8. The copy has direct action objectives.

9. The firm has no salespeople or dealers.

10. The ad wants to generate high-quality inquiries.

11. The copy is directed to people who do not use the product at present.

12. The firm is introducing a brand into a highly competitive market.

MAKING LONG COPY LOOK INVITING

In addition to being interesting, long copy should be made to look easy to read. Proper graphic and typographical treatment can go a long way toward facilitating reading and giving an appearance of easy reading. Here are a few techniques that have been proven effective:

1. Use short paragraphs that are indented, not flush, with double spacing between each, and occasionally centered. Make judicious use of italics, caps, boldface, or oversize initials or caps.

2. Copy blocks should not be too wide for proper eye range in relation to the size of the type; vary widths; graduate the type sizes starting with the larger sizes and dropping to the smaller.

3. Use frequent subheadlines. Make them bold enough to break up any body copy that appears too formidable, but don't make them so frequent or so bold that they will distract the reader from the consequential flow of the copy message. Consider the use of a two- or three-sentence introduction and display subheads between

the headline and the opening body matter to get the reader into the first paragraph of text.

4. Use a type size that is consistent with the copy length you have decided on to accomplish your objective. Remember that if you hold interest, people will read much smaller type, thus enabling you to get more sales angles into your ad than you ever imagined.

5. Use as much white space as possible that is consistent with your objective. Remember, however, although some amount of white space will help you get attention, every unnecessary line of it deletes copy that would be more likely to gain your objective than the white space.

6. Use artwork to advance or substantiate the copy message—not for mere decoration. Again, the amount of space that the artwork occupies, if it is any degree unnecessary, eats up space that the copy could be occupying to produce greater results.

7. Product specifications, sizes, power required, and so on, can sometimes be set in smaller type and boxed off from the main copy. These points are there for those who want to know them, but they should not interfere with the more attractive display of your main message containing motivational copy.

COPY THAT INFORMS

Again speaking generally, copy is usually longer for prospects and shorter for present users. People now using your product are apt to know what the benefits are, what it provides, how efficiently it performs, what it can be used for, and where it may be purchased. Prospects may know practically none of these things. They may have never even heard about your product. The copy to this audience would have to be highly informative. Also, industrial advertising copy is usually more effective when it is rather long and informative because the reader (in this case, possibly the purchasing agent) wants to know:

1. What the product is doing for other companies under similar conditions.

2. What design or engineering features make it suitable for meeting the company's needs for solving problems.

3. What is involved in the area of installation and any problems that might occur.

4. Requirements for proper maintenance.

5. Costs and periods of time required for the product to pay for itself.

Fairly long copy is generally needed in these situations and should be carefully considered. It will stand a good chance of being read if it is interesting, looks inviting, is well organized, and is well developed.

WHEN TO CONSIDER SHORT COPY

Short copy is used in situations where it is not warranted more often than the other way around. Here are a few of the principal conditions where short copy would be appropriate:

1. The ad is concerned with convenience goods.

2. The product is of simple construction, use, or maintenance.

3. The brand is not sufficiently differentiated.

4. The product provides only a trifling benefit.

5. The product is very low priced.

6. The copy will be used in radio or television commercials.

7. The copy is to be used in outdoor media.

8. The copy will appear on transit cards (in buses, taxicabs, and the like).

9. The objective is to develop a favorable attitude toward your brand.

10. You have indirect action objectives.

11. The bulk of the sales work is done by salespeople and dealers.

12. You are seeking a maximum number of inquiries.

13. The ad is directed to people who are present users of your product.

14. Your firm and your brand are long established and have widespread user acceptance.

THE BODY TEXT

Experienced advertising writers usually know what they wish to say before they start to put it on paper. They will have drafted a complete ad in their minds and will experiment with headlines and illustration ideas for it. After selecting the best of their many ideas and when an interesting picture or illustration idea is chosen, the writers are ready to write the body copy. The importance of this part of the ad cannot be overemphasized. The picture calls attention; the headline sparks an interest and curiosity. Together, they convey the information and contribute to the readers' desire to own the product or partake of the service. In the majority of effective advertising, the headline and illustration simply open the door for the customers; it is the body copy that usually clinches the buying decision. The beginning writer who wishes to approach perfection should practice diligently to accomplish three things in his or her writing: (1) arouse unusual interest, (2) convey complete conviction, and (3) create great desire.

SEQUENCE OF IDEAS

The ideas in any body copy should be expressed in proper sequence. Broadly, this means obeying the cliche, "Don't put the cart before the horse." The readers should not be urged to buy until they have been given some good reasons why they should want the product, and the reasons should be set down in as logical an order as possible.

DIFFERENT WAYS IN WHICH BODY COPY MAY BE WRITTEN

In some advertising textbooks it is customary to divide body text into several classifications such as "reason why" copy, human interest copy, descriptive copy, and the like.

In actual practice, the experienced advertising writer rarely selects a classification in advance and writes copy to conform to that. Rather, he or she strives to give it the three basic requirements—unusual interest, complete conviction, and great persuasion. With these requirements in mind, the writer begins to write. When the text is finished, it may fall into any one of the classifications given in the textbooks or be a combination of two or more of them. He or she may be serious, thoughtful, romantic, emotional, light, or humorous; positive or negative; narrative or expository; descriptive or inferential.

One hears a great deal about "reason why" copy, yet there seems to be no precise general agreement as to exactly what it means. Some people say that reason why copy is copy that simply appeals to reason; others say it is copy that presents factual reasons why people should buy the product. Some others say that it is argumentative copy that seeks to present arguments so logical that the readers will accept and act upon it.

Another kind of copy is called "human interest" copy, but, here again, the definition is fuzzy. Some people say that human interest copy appeals to the emotions. Our distinction, however, presupposes that reason why copy can have no emotional appeal in it whereas human interest copy must be lacking in reason why. This is fallacious reasoning. An insurance ad that urges spouses and parents to protect the future of their families by taking out insurance uses an emotional appeal in its human interest copy, but it also gives one of the most cogent reasons for buying insurance and so it is really reason why copy too.

As you sit down to write, you may wonder whether the words should be serious, light, or humorous; this depends mainly on whether you can see your product in one of those lights. No writer in his or her right mind would attempt to be humorous when writing about cemetery lots. On the other hand, some national advertisers, such as Sanka Coffee, have treated their product both seriously and humorously. The same is true, over a period of years, for Travelers Insurance Company, which has ranged from light to serious, from humorous to thoughtful, and from descriptive to informative. What Travelers is looking for in its copy is not whether it is reason why or human interest, but that it poses a problem to all readers and then offers a solution to the problem that is satisfying, both financially and emotionally.

SYMBOLS AND SYMBOLISM

Symbols and symbolic illustrations can be extremely useful in advertising. Sometimes a symbol can be used to picture an idea that can be otherwise difficult to illustrate. A symbol may be used to emphasize a need or selling point. Symbolic illustrations can be used to heighten dramatic effect, express an idea, or illustrate an abstract idea. For instance, if you have a product that goes into airplanes, then you can truthfully say that it is on "most of the world's leading airlines." An interesting way to illustrate "most of the world's leading airlines" is to show all the caps worn by the airline pilots (symbols), which makes an attractive array with the name of each airline printed beneath the caps. If you are talking about worldwide distribution, we have seen the same thing done with small representations of flags, which is very appealing. If you say you are a supplier to many of the country's leading manufac-

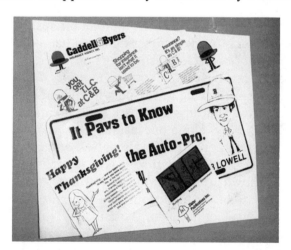

Figure 7-2. Symbols in ad logos. (Used with permission of Caddell & Byers Insurance Agency, Inc., 21 George St., Lowell, MA 01852; Bournival World of Transportation, 831 Rogers St., Lowell, MA 01852; and Slater Publications, Inc., 1502 Providence Highway, Norwood, MA 02062.)

turers, an array of their logos can be interesting, if arranged in an attractive manner. Other examples of symbols that have been employed with considerable success include the "little girl" (everything nice) illustration used to soften the image of a small-town bank, and a variety of "hat" symbols used for such diverse clients as a publisher and an insurance agency. (See Fig. 7-2.)

THE USE OF DIAGRAMS

When preparing your ad, you're not exclusively working with words or pictures. Try to think of everything available. One good device is diagrams, which make things clearer, more interesting, more convincing, or more provocative. For instance, if you were creating an ad for prefabricated houses, it would be a good idea to display a picture of the finished product in a beautiful setting showing how lovely and conventional your prefabricated house appears, but it would certainly increase interest and be more informative if you included a supplementary illustration of a floor plan of the house. In addition, you increase conviction if you choose supplementary illustrations that show prefabricated sections being erected. The idea is the most important part of all.

Again, it should be emphasized that the subject matter is more important than the technique. In arriving at an illustration idea for an ad, the important thing to decide is what the picture should portray. For example, suppose you are working with a rather abstract headline like "The greater the skill, the better the job," and this headline is addressed primarily to sports enthusiasts. Since baseball has almost universal sports appeal, the subject matter suggested in the illustration could be an outfielder catching a fly ball. Once the subject matter is decided upon, you can determine, with the art director, what is the most interesting way to show it pictorially. You might decide to get a news shot or stock photo of some big league outfielder making a very dramatic catch; you may decide to have an artist make an interesting painting of this subject; perhaps you decide to use some famous historical catch done in a "Believe-It-or-Not" style; or maybe you decide to have a cartoonist draw a goofy-looking outfielder who is running with outstretched arms as the ball bounces off his head. Before you get into the technique, however, you must decide what will make the most captivating subject matter for your illustration. And, once again, it all boils down to the creative concept clearly and concisely portrayed.

SELECTING THE PUBLICATION

There are, of course, many other considerations involved in your space ad program; for example, the number of different ads you need to create, if color should be used, what size ad is most cost-effective for your purposes, and what publication would best reach your target audience. Choosing the right publication is of prime importance. As mentioned elsewhere, the *Standard Rate & Data Services* (*SRDS*) (See Chapter 1) is a series of directories that include information on practically every publication in the United States and Canada. Different volumes include Radio, TV, Business Publications, Agricultural Publications, and even one for Direct Mail Lists and Response Cards.

After you have looked up the market area in which you are interested and found the publications reaching your target market in the *SRDS,* your next step is to get in touch with the publication rep from the magazine and have him or her send you the "media kit" for that particular publication. This material should include a rate card, an audit statement, and a complete breakdown of circulation readership studies, demographics, and other pertinent details. (See Fig.7–3.)

Figure 7–3. Media kits. (Used with permission of CW Publishing, Inc., 375 Cochituate Rd., Framingham, MA 01701.)

In order to determine the most effective publication, you might ask the rep some of the following questions:

1. How does your circulation match the target audience I am interested in reaching?

2. Do our competitors or companies with similar products and services advertise in the publication?

3. Is this "paid" (purchased by subscribers) or "free" (sent without charge to qualifying readers)?

4. Are there special issues that may relate specifically to my product or service, and are there any extra issues and copies distributed at trade shows?

5. Does the publication have a new product or new literature section that may accept my publicity releases?

6. Has the publication circulation and advertising revenue been increasing or decreasing over recent years?

7. Is this book audited? (Ask for the BPA or ABP audit statement; see Fig. 7–4.)

Figure 7-4. BPA audit statement. (Used with permission of *Business Publications Audit,* 360 Park Avenue South, New York, NY 10010.)

8

Electronic Media: Radio, Television, Telemarketing, and Outdoor Advertising

RADIO AND TELEVISION

Radio and television are included in the classification of major advertising media along with newspapers, magazines, direct mail, and outdoor advertising, however, relatively few manufacturers or distributors of industrial goods turn to either radio or TV. Instead, these two media generally attract the marketers of consumer goods or the operators of retail outlets—local, regional, or national. We have also placed telemarketing in this chapter, although this most recently utilized medium resembles direct marketing programs. Among other benefits, it can provide impressive quantities of sales leads.

Beyond the fact that outdoor or billboard advertising often utilizes lighting (lighted boards), we have no real reason to include it in this particular chapter. In fact, outdoor advertising most resembles space or publication advertising in that the number of exposures in a given territory are measured to determine the rate that is usually commissionable to the ad agency.

Consumer goods communication managers working with modest budgets frequently add radio to their advertising schedules, but TV usually remains beyond their modest reach.

For a number of years, television stood as the third most important medium from the point of view of dollars involved. It trailed newspapers and direct mail. In the early 1980s, TV took over second place behind newspapers, and we feel, if it hasn't happened already, TV will be the medium in which the largest number of promotional dollars will be invested.

You might be tempted to consider television for your advertising program—tempted, that is, until you learn the brutal cost story. To start, you must first produce your commercial. The average cost of producing a thirty-second, professional-type commercial of which you can be proud runs about $70,000. Many local advertisers have had ads (some fair but mostly poor) produced for them at significantly lower costs. In the main, however, these minimum-cost efforts lack the professional touch and the professional results.

If you feel you would like to explore TV-land, one way to get a feel for production costs is to sit down with a representative from your local TV station. He or she can quote you figures and handle the making of the commercial for you. This is the low-cost way to go. Should you approach an independent TV production house, then you start to talk big money.

Both radio and TV use the broad "buckshot" approach when airing their message. With either, your commercial reaches every ear tuned to the station. Unfortunately, as in the case of most industrial items, relatively few of the listeners qualify as valid prospects even though the total audience is large. But the advertiser has to pay a bundle to reach a vast audience, unprofitable as most of them may be. That suggests, of course, that industrial goods marketers should take a "rifle" approach, with advertising directed only at legitimate prospects through media such as direct mail and specialized business magazines.

COST CONSIDERATIONS

As you explore the costs of possibly using radio or television or both in your promotional program, you'll find a great variance. Naturally, the medium will charge top dollar when it has its top audience. We know this as *prime time*.

Time segments (or *day parts*) carry significantly different price tags. Not too many years back, both radio and television felt that the evening hours between 6:00 and 11:00 qualified for the prime time (and most costly) label. Listenership studies have changed that paleolithic thinking. Radio now correctly considers the hours between 6:00 and 8:00 A.M. and 4:00 and 6:00 P.M. to be prime. These are drive-time hours—millions of cars are on the road and virtually every one is equipped with a radio. And, after turning on the ignition, almost every driver turns on the radio. Most people seem to feel that the car won't move if the radio is not operating.

Obviously, then, drive-time has become radio's prime time. You will pay four to five times as much for a commercial broadcast during those time segments than you will at other parts of the day or night.

The usual radio commercial runs for one minute. This contrasts with the most popular TV commercial which runs for one-half minute. That one-minute commercial on radio can cost as little as $15 or as much as $500 to $600, depending on a couple of factors.

The first, of course, is the time segment—the day part during which you wish your message to be broadcast. Prime time or drive time costs you more than any other hour you might select.

Furthermore, the station's signal strength has a significant bearing on the charges. The Federal Communications Commission (watchdog of the airways) permits stations to go on the air with specific power limits. Relatively few of the AM stations receive licenses to operate on the maximum strength of 50,000 watts. (These are the clear channel stations.) Many smaller local stations are permitted to broadcast only at 1,000 watts. Obviously, the more powerful stations reach many more persons and that means higher costs to the advertiser.

When you buy a one-minute commercial on a 50,000-watt station at prime time, you will obviously pay top dollar. That same one-minute advertisement running at 10:00 P.M. on a 1,000-watt station will make only a small dent in your promotional budget. Of course, the commercial on the weak station will not deliver your message to many prospects, but you will hit some, which will provide a base from which you can build.

The Standard Rate & Data Service, which provides you with a rate book for newspapers and magazines, also has a volume that covers every radio station in the country. From this you can quickly find the cost and the strength of any radio station that interests you. (Refer to *SRDS* in Chapter 1.)

All of the major media have established information offices designed to help advertisers who might have an interest in a specific medium. In the case of radio, for example, an inquiry directed to the

Radio Advertising Bureau, 485 Lexington Avenue, New York, NY 10017, will enable you to learn more about radio as a medium than you care to know. Television's counterpart, the Television Advertising Bureau, is located at 477 Madison Avenue, New York, NY 10022.

RADIO'S STRENGTHS AND WEAKNESSES

As mentioned earlier, small budget advertisers (retailers and manufacturers) buy most of the radio time. And, they come back to it, month after month, because it works. Radios are ubiquitous. You find them in factories, offices, homes, autos, on beaches, on joggers, ad infinitum. The average adult listens to radio in excess of three hours a day. The radio may be listened to while an individual participates in other activities—washing a car, cleaning the house, eating dinner, doing all sorts of routine jobs. Radio can also enable you to address a selective audience even though, at first blush, it seems to talk to everyone. Today's stations have developed programming designed to appeal primarily to men or women, to teenagers or golden agers, to pop music fans or classical music lovers, to all-talk shows, all-news shows, or all-sports shows—all kind of formats, appealing to all kinds of audiences.

Because radio costs relatively little, the advertiser with a reasonable budget can enjoy both reach and frequency when airing his or her messages. So, it provides a bit of the best of several worlds.

However, the low cost can contribute to one of radio's major weaknesses—clutter. The modest price tag motivates many low-budget advertisers to use the radio, which often contributes to listeners' major gripe—"too much advertising."

Further, the proliferation of radio stations in any given geographical area leads to audience fragmentation. Boston residents can receive over *thirty* radio stations loudly and clearly. When you take into consideration the fact that some eight to ten VHF and UHF TV stations, along with a rich cable fare, are all on the air at the same time, you can rest assured that mighty few individuals are tuned to a number of the weaker radio outlets.

Many advertisers exclude radio from their schedules because it features audio only. They feel they want to show their products, trademarks, packages, or results of using their products. They can do this on TV, in newspapers, magazines, and direct mail, but not radio.

Mail order marketers who rely on the use of coupons or the memorization of a telephone number do not usually turn to radio. One fast growing trend, however, designed to assist consumers in recalling phone numbers they hear on radio, is the number acronym. If you can persuade the telephone company to provide you with a series of numbers that spells out a word or two, you will benefit. For example, if you own an insurance agency, you would be way ahead of the pack if you could tell listeners, "Just dial 555-SAFE."

One promotional idea that works well with both the radio and the TV advertiser is to print on package and store display material, "As Heard on Radio" or "As Seen on TV." Those magic words seem to add considerable credibility to the company's offering.

TV'S STRENGTHS AND WEAKNESSES

Of all the media available to you, the most potent is television. With its ability to combine sight and sound, it provides you with a fairly effective substitute for a live salesperson. TV can talk about a product and its virtues, demonstrate how to use the product, and show the results of using or not using it.

The major drawback of this medium is, of course, the high cost. Few small- or even medium-sized firms have the financial resources to sustain an on-going, effective promotional campaign on television.

KINDS OF COMMERCIALS

The Straight Commercial

A straight radio commercial uses one voice unassisted by any devices. It contains no sound effects and no special musical efforts. Its interest and appeal depends on what is said and the way it is said. If the straight commercial is well written and if it fulfills the five functions of an ad, its interest can be heightened by the pleasing quality of the announcer's voice punctuated by sincerity, enthusiasm, and inflection. Conversely, if the commercial is dull in its writing, it will be dull in its delivery despite the talents of the announcer. In a straight television commercial the appearance of the spokesperson becomes as important as his or her voice, perhaps even more so. Unfortunately or fortunately, people are apt to form likes and dislikes on appearance alone, before the person even opens his or her mouth.

The Dialog Commercial

In radio, the dialog commercial is two or more voices that are heard talking to each other. Bob and Ray are an example of a marvelous long-running duo. Both have done humor of their own and have done many humorous commercials.

In television, it is two or more people who are both seen and heard talking to each other. A dialog commercial may consist of one person asking questions about the product and the other answering—it could be a person asking a druggist or asking a clerk about a product; it could be a person asking a mechanic in the repair section of an automotive shop for advice; or it may be a discussion of a product when each person who speaks emphasizes some special sales point.

The Conversational Commercial

The conversational commercial is not what the name implies; it is not a conversation between two people. In radio and television, it is a message given by one announcer, but instead of a smooth reading or an uninterrupted delivery, the announcer seems to be ad libbing. The individual appears to be talking across the table to the listener concerning whatever comes into his or her mind rather than delivering a message that has been prepared in advance.

The Device Commercial

A device commercial may be set up as an unusual situation with the product introduced in a surprising but logical way. It may be a very short musical production, a dramatic incident, or it may simply be the introduction of a sound effect. In a radio commercial, it might be an ambulance siren.

The Dramatized Commercial

The dramatized commercial is usually a short incident that contains a plot. A problem is presented and it is resolved by the product. For example, Julie refuses to date Jerome because of his appearance; Jerome gets "Glop" and his appearance changes; and girl dates boy.

The Corny Commercial

The corny commercial is human, homespun, and folksy. It permits more feeling and emotion about a product than would be natural with a sophisticated announcer. With the right announcer, this type of commercial can be magnificent, which means very corny!

The Animated Commercial

In radio, an animated commercial is one that uses different voices augmented by sound or musical effects. For example, suppose a testimonial letter has to be read as part of the commercial. On a straight commercial, the announcer would say, "I would like to read a letter from Mrs. Macaroon from Daytona Beach." The announcer would then proceed to read the letter. On an animated commercial, the announcer might say, "Here's a letter from way down in Dixie. It's from Mrs. Macaroon! She says. . . ." Then a woman's voice would read the testimonial, perhaps while an orchestra plays background music as the testimonial is being read.

On television, an animated commercial allows for a great deal of flexibility, such as dancing cigarettes, flying hamburgers, or any inanimate object put in motion. A cartoon commercial in which the figures move and speak is an animated commercial.

The following is a sample of a radio script as sent to a local radio station on behalf of a client in the auto agency business. This is a sixty-second script to be read by the station announcer. Other spots in this same series include thirty-second versions as well as some calling for two voices, which require special outside talent and a taping session.

◀——————————————————————————————

## Sample:	Radio Script*

Auto Dealer Client

Radio Script

General Full Line

February 20, 19-- to "TIL FORBID"

60 seconds

SFX: (Swish, Swish, Swish—sound of golf club through the air)

ANNOUNCER:
There he goes again . . . Dick Bournival, the "Auto Pro" . . . Bournival Chrysler Plymouth, Route 495 at Route 38 Lowell . . . polishing up his golf game and his "Bournivalues" on every single vehicle on display . . . Plymouths, Chryslers, Mazdas, Winnebagos . . . used cars and trucks . . . everything now at tremendous savings! That's right! TREMENDOUS SAVINGS ON EVERYTHING!!! That's why we outsell the others and that's why we say, "Don't even think of buying before you see Bournival." AND, because Bournival is New England's Number One Chrysler, Plymouth, Mazda, and Winnebago dealer, you not only get the lowest, rock-bottom prices, but you get a huge selection from which to choose. So, come on over and see the "Auto Pros" at Bournival. They're easy to reach, right at Exit 38 . . . junction of Routes 38 and 495. Don't miss the "Auto Pro" when he's in a swinging, selling mood. Come to Bournival, where it pays to know the "Auto Pro." (Fade out from echo chamber.) Bournival, where it pays to know the "Auto Pro," Bournival, where it pays to know the "Auto Pro."

-30-

——————————————————————————————▶

*Used with permission of Bournival World of Transportation, 831 Rogers St., Lowell, MA 01852.

RADIO STATIONS THAT ACCEPT PER INQUIRY
(PI) ADVERTISING

Many radio and TV stations operate what is known as the PI (per inquiry) advertising system. This kind of operation allows the station to obtain income from unsponsored time. Various sales operations, especially in the mail order operations field, have found this radio PI advertising an economical and profitable method to enter a given market.

All kinds of products have been advertised in this kind of set up, but as a rule, they are items with good markup, thus enabling the advertiser to offer a good commission to the station on each item. The most appealing aspect of such a plan is that the advertiser has little initial expenditure in getting the product before the public since he or she pays only for the orders actually received from the station. Most stations' general pattern is to run night radio shows with various spots strategically placed throughout various time periods.

The list of stations subscribing to the per inquiry promotions seems to grow each year, which shows the immense popularity of the technique. PI stations are looking for products to sell, and it is good business to give them what they want. By means of such advertising, you will be able to locate markets for your product that you did not know existed and that would not be uncovered in the ordinary course of sales and advertising efforts. Your offer will be exposed to buyers who might not be sold by any other method. Some stations of 500,000 watts operating on a twenty-four-hour schedule are known to pull orders from almost every state in the union. Even the smaller stations pay off in a big way.

How do you go about contacting radio stations regarding per inquiry advertising? The first thing to keep in mind is that you are initiating a business proposition. Do not impose on the station's advertising editor's time and patience by sending him or her long pages of praise of your product and company. Make sure that you have something to say—and say it. Forget the flowery language and the phrases to sell! Give the gist of your proposition as meaty and fact-packed as possible. The advertising editor will select what he or she thinks the station's listeners want to know. The best way, of course, is to listen to a number of programs emanating from the station you are interested in contacting and find out exactly what other advertisers have to say. Keep your informational release short and factual, and do not attempt to take a sideswipe at competitors.

The following steps are guidelines designed to help you promote your product for PI advertising by the aid of radio stations:

1. The first page, which should be typed on your business letterhead, should be a letter to the *advertising editor.* Describe your product in the letter and give reasons why you believe it would sell to the listeners. Do not go into great detail on the merits of your item but refer the editor instead to an enclosed press release.

2. Offer the station a generous commission on each order it gets for you; state the exact amount for each order (usually from 30 to 50 percent). Inform how you will pay (daily, weekly, or monthly). Given the name of your local bank and the person there to contact.

3. If possible, show that your advertising gets results. Let the station know if you have advertised on radio, in magazines, in newspapers, or other media.

4. In your press release, tell first about your business and then about the appealing features of your product. Cover every interesting angle—height, weight, breadth, shipping weight, color, and the like. Cite your financial situation as proof of your ability to make good on unsatisfactory merchandise. Assure the editor that your merchandise will sell on a mass basis and that it has wide appeal and can stand competition.

5. If possible, include a free sample of your product with your letter and release. This will give the editor an opportunity to examine your product first hand and determine the validity of the claims you want him or her to air on behalf of your product. Be sure to state that you will refund money to any radio listener who is not satisfied.

6. On a separate sheet of paper, write the copy you wish the station to run. This copy is extremely important since everything depends on how well it will evoke a desire to buy. It is imperative that the listeners be encouraged to act at once—not a day from now, not an hour from now, but at that precise moment. If you do not force the listeners to get a pencil and paper right away, the chances are they will forget the address, and you will lose orders.

7. Finally, when a station responds by requesting more details, answer at once!

What stations should be sent the product information release? In a great measure, this will be predetermined by the nature of your product. Just as good mail-order promoters study the editorial content and reading habits of the people who buy the magazine they plan to advertise in, so should radio advertisers study the policies of the various radio stations. Some of the questions you should consider are: To what type audience are the programs being beamed? Are they the best prospects for this type of merchandise?

Don't expect every station to accept your PI offer! Some may not have open time; others may not be sold on your product or may not be satisfied with the commission you offer them; and still others may be selling a similar item now and are not interested in competitive products.

PREPARING TV COMMERCIALS

As pointed out, writing TV copy is quite similar in many respects to writing radio scripts. Where they differ, of course, is in the visual aspects required by television that need not be contended with in radio. This visualization of the TV commercial is communicated by means of a pictorial outline called a *storyboard*.

Figure 8-1. Storyboard form and radio script. (Used with permission of Dennison Manufacturing Company, 275 Wyman St., Waltham, MA 02154.)

Storyboards usually take the form of mini-TV squares or frames that are used to indicated high points of the visual action of the TV storyline. Right beside each frame is a section for copy or audio part, which also runs along with the action of the commercial. (See Fig. 8–1.)

The following TV spot was produced for a real estate firm. Rather than live action, a series of slides were used to showcase the area being promoted. The slides moved or were changed with a cue from the announcer's voice-over script.

◀───

Sample: TV Script Sheet

TELEVISION COPY

Television Media Group, Inc.

Sponsor: _____   Program & Station: _____
Number & Product: _____   Date: _____   Length: ____

VIDEO	SCENE #	AUDIO
Live talent #	open	Only 25 minutes from down-
ANNCR	SLIDE #1	town Ft. Lauderdale on Route
VOICE OVER		1, Sunnyfield is one of the
		fastest growing communities
		in Florida. Indeed, it is one of
		the most attractive communi-
		ties in the entire state. Run by
	SLIDE #2	Town Meeting, Sunnyfield
		has a population of over
	SLIDE #3	40,000, with an excellent pub-
		lic transportation system. The
	SLIDE #4	public school system is also
		excellent, with a pupil/teacher
		ratio of about 21 to 1. It has
	SLIDE #5	eight elementary, three mid-
		dle, and two senior high
		schools, as well as a superior

SLIDE #6	vocational school. The hospital is in the town and shopping facilities are superb, both downtown and in the famous Sunnyfield mall.
LOGO SLIDE	Sunnyfield Brochure (Close-up of address) (Close-up of telephone number)
LOGO WITH TAG	For more information and a free brochure, call or write today.

_____ ▶

MERCHANDISING TELEVISION PROMOTIONS

In addition to including "As Seen on TV" or "As Heard on Radio" on your packaging and in your ads, as mentioned earlier, storyboards may also serve as merchandising aids when they are reconstructed and printed in full color, for example.

TELEMARKETING

We have arbitrarily included telemarketing in this chapter on electronic media. It could just as well have been placed in our chapter on direct mail since it involves the rifle-shot approach or the individual one-on-one promotion to a well-defined potential market. We have used telemarketing both as a research tool and a promotional vehicle. In both cases, we have found that using an outside telemarketing resource is far more efficient and effective than trying to do this type of telephone work inside a regularly functioning office environment.

The few times we attempted to do an in-house telemarketing program we ran into so much confusion and phone tie-ups that we now recommend an outside telemarketing operation for all, except the smallest size efforts of this kind. We find that an outside resource is far better equipped to provide the supervision, professional motivation, script development, and overall implementation of most types of telephone programs.

In addition, an outside telemarketing resource will provide the most current and automated telecommunication systems, utilizing a network of equipment and lines to measure and maximize productivity. It can also provide a more efficient work environment, including work stations, noise control, and so on, which is unavailable in the usual in-house operation. Finally, the account executive from a telemarketing firm provides the supervision and control that we found hard to maintain within an inside office system.

The following is a list of services provided by a professional telemarketing operation. Use this as a checklist of elements needed to achieve your telemarketing goals.

Business-to-Business Telemarketing Capabilities
Outbound Calling
- Lead Generation
- Lead Qualifying
- Product and Service Sales
- Information Gathering
- Market Surveying (Research)
- Customer Service

Inbound Service
- Product Ordering
- Lead Generation
- Requests for Information
- Literature Fulfillment

Business-to-Consumer Telemarketing Capabilities
- Direct Mail Follow Up
- Lead Generation
- Product and Service Sales
- Financial Services
- Subscription Sales
- Customer Service

A SUCCESSFUL TELEMARKETING PROGRAM

The following steps will help you in planning a successful telemarketing program for your product or service.

1. *Project Overview:* The first step in implementing a successful tele-marketing program is to understand the scope and desired goal of the project. You must be able to state clearly how the telemarketing program integrates with the overall marketing plan of the company.

2. *Target Goals:* A results-oriented telemarketing program is based on establishing realistic, measurable, and achievable results. Although projects of different scopes will vary in the type of expected results, each project must be constantly monitored from launch to completion.

3. *Script Development:* Script development and implementation is essential to the success of your telemarketing program. Scripting is not a static element in that once the script is developed, it must be tested prior to the project's full implementation. Also, scripts should be contantly monitored and modified as needed to achieve the desired results.

4. *Project Staffing:* Staffing for each project is as individual as the project's other requirements. Telephone communicators should be different individuals with varying skills. Some projects call for a strong sales approach; others do not. For example, a different personality would be required for customer service than for market information surveys.

5. *Constant Monitoring:* Once the project is active, the original goals should be maintained. Constant monitoring of objectives and performance keeps the project on track to maximize results.

6. *Project Reporting:* Results must be reported at periodic intervals as well as at project completion. Compiled statistical information on project results should be arranged in a clear, concise manner, employing charts and graphs wherever they can assist understanding.

The following is a detailed breakdown of a research project conducted through a telemarketing firm to determine the impressions of attendees at the Business-to-Business Expo trade show. The telemarketing company handled all the operational details of the survey, such as script development, training of communicators, monitoring and rebriefing telephone operators, and management reports, and provided the raw data in hard copy and on floppy disks for assimilation into our final report to the client.

RESEARCH OBJECTIVES

Whether you use an outside telemarketing operation or perform the telemarketing in-house, the first step in any telemarketing research, or for that matter, any kind of telemarketing program, will be to state your objectives clearly and get them down on paper. The survey below was conducted along these lines.

A. Survey Objectives:
  1. Describe the attendees' experiences at and their resulting attitudes about the Business-to-Business Expo show.
  2. Provide the preceding information in a way that would be useful to The Producers in planning future shows.

B. Information Needs:
  1. A description of attendees' attitudes regarding the types of products and services exhibited at the show.
  2. A determination of whether the attendees encountered exhibitors with which they could possibly transact business but would not have encountered through other business channels such as trade publications.
  3. A determination of the participation in, and reaction to, the seminars held at the show.
  4. A measure of the attitudes toward the show as a whole as reflected by their statements regarding their willingness to recommend the show to others and the value that they would place on an admission price to the show.

The data were to be collected from respondents who had filled out registration forms in order to attend the Business-to-Business Expo.

DATA COLLECTION METHOD

The data collection method selected for this survey was the telephone interview. The principal consideration in choosing the telephone method was the need to have the survey administered quickly before the attendees forgot much of their show experiences and the attitudes that they held at that time.

SAMPLING ACTIVITIES

The set of forms were screened prior to data collection activity. The purpose of the screening was to assign to certain registrant forms priority in the survey process. Two criteria were used in identifying the "priority" aspects: the title of the registrant's position and the name recognition of the organization. Priority was given to those forms that suggested executive-level positions within large organizations with a high level of name awareness among the business community.

The survey was administered by telephone within two weeks after the trade show. Based on leads furnished by the client, the results of the sampling activity were:

Total Calls Attempted	159
Number of Contacts	93
Number of Completed Surveys	88

The difference between the Total Calls Attempted and the Number of Completed Surveys is attributable to many factors, including wrong telephone numbers, duplicate leads, and no answers. Of the 93 contacts made, 88 (96 percent) agreed to participate in the survey.

The following is the final analysis as presented to the client, along with questionnaire tabulations, respondent characteristics, sampling activities, and original tally sheets. The results of the survey were reported in the following brief summary:

Executive Summary

Responses from a telephone interview of 88 attendees at the Business-to-Business Expo suggest that the show overall was a success. The general attitude about the show was positive. Eighty percent said they would recommend attendance to colleagues.

The attendees regarded the Expo as a good opportunity to review new companies and perhaps meet with other firms with whom they otherwise would never have come in contact.

For the most part, the attendees were satisfied with the variety of the exhibitors, with a considerable percentage (73 percent) saying that the products and services they found at the show were useful for their organization. A cursory review of the comments in the questionnaires suggested that there may be room for improvement regarding the quality of individual exhibitors; there were several spontaneous comments regarding annoyance at encountering unmanned booths.

Some interesting areas for The Producers to give considerable thought to were: (1) the seminars and (2) the issue of an admission fee. Ninety percent indicated that they did not attend the seminars, and almost all of them suggested that time was the impediment. Half (56 percent) of the respondents would be willing to pay no more than $5 to attend the show, with the rest generally willing to pay up to $10; the data suggest that the price they had in mind applies only to attendance at the exhibition area and not at the seminars.

Telemarketing Project Cost

PROJECT COST

	Option A	Option B
Number of Completed Surveys	100	200
Number of Completed Surveys per Hour	3	3
Total Calling Hours	34	67
Cost per Hour	$ 27.50	$ 27.50
Total Calling Cost	$ 935.00	$1,842.50
Start Up and Preparation Fee (which includes preliminary program development, reserving production time, and training costs for supervisory and telephone sales personnel) Development of Script/ Conversation Guide Design of Lead Form (for client access to original data and to maintain discipline in	$ 500.00	$ 500.00

	Option A	*Option B*
the production environment)		
Total Project Cost	$1,435.00	$2,342.50
Carrier, Delivery or Fax Service (as needed)	At Cost	At Cost
Clerical Costs (nonproduction-related, i.e., affixing pressure-sensitive labels to lead forms, sending fulfillment materials, etc.)	$14.00/Hour	$14.00/Hour
Required Deposit (remainder net 30 days)	$ 500.00	$ 820.00

OUTDOOR ADVERTISING

Outdoor advertising (billboards) provide yet another, though diminishing, way to promote your product or service. This medium provides a unique manner to make a selective approach to a given physical area of your marketplace. It delivers unmatched frequency, since it is visible all day every day, showing your message over and over. And it does not let your customer forget your sales message—it cannot be turned off or thrown away. Although the availability of outdoor billboards has decreased steadily over the years, it still represents a good cost-effective buy in most major market areas.

There are two popular sizes for billboards. One is the poster panel, sometimes called the 30-sheet poster, which runs 12 feet by 25 feet. The second most popular size is the painted bulletin, a giant 14 feet by 48 feet painted board which requires more artwork and far more extensive production costs. There are other sizes, shapes, and designs of outdoor bulletins and billboards, and you can check availabilities and sizes, as well as overall production cost, with your local outdoor advertising display representative.

Billboards are usually purchased by "showings" and it is wise to look at the actual locations in order to make sure that your message is placed precisely where you wish.

The following is a typical "showing," which includes all the facts about the boards in this particular grouping. In addition, the outdoor advertising broker will also include a set of demographics that provides a fairly accurate breakdown of the kinds of people who will see the board and how often they will view it.

#10 Daily Gross Rating point (33 Boards) Poster Showing

The Medium:	Poster panels (12 ′ × 25 ′)
The Market:	Baltimore/Washington, DC metro
Total Daily Circulation:	Total adults: 460,000
Net Reach Monthly:	Total adults: 48.8%
Average Monthly Frequency:	4.9
Duration:	30 days
Units:	33 (11 regular, 22 illuminated)
Copy:	Advertiser to supply; mechanical to be prepared in scale of 1/2″ to 1 ′ (based on 9 ′9 ″ to 21 ′)
Cost per Thousand Impressions:	$ 1.12
Cost Per GRP (Gross Rating Points):	$ 51.61
Cost per Month:	$12,342.00

Market: Baltimore/Washington, DC

Population: 4,525,500

Showing: #10 (11 regular, 22 illuminated)

Demographic:	Reach (%)	Frequency
Adults	44.6	4.6 times
Men	56.3	4.3 times
Women	47.3	3.8 times
Adults 18 to 34	52.7	4.9 times
Adults 35 to 49	58.4	3.5 times
Adults 50 +	51.1	2.9 times
Adults Upper Income	63.1	4.2 times
Adults Middle Income	63.0	3.8 times
Adults Low Income	57.4	3.8 times
Teens 14 to 17	43.8	4.2 times
Men 18 to 34	66.4	4.5 times
Men 35 to 49	62.4	3.8 times
Men 50 +	53.1	3.2 times

Women 18 to 34	67.0	3.3 times
Women 35 to 49	59.4	2.9 times
Women 50 +	52.2	2.5 times

Daily Effective Circulation: 450,000
Average Effective Circulation per Poster Panel:
    Illuminated: 17,200
    Unilluminated: 7,300

One very important factor when looking at billboards is that they are a totally different medium from others that we have discussed. Billboards are meant to be seen on the fly—that is, from a moving automobile—and therefore must be created differently from a space ad. A billboard is a sign. And, as such, you must remember to keep the copy short. Eleven words is probably a rule of thumb average maximum billboard copy length.

Additionally, remember that the artwork has to be reformatted entirely if you are to adapt it from a space ad. We remember in one instance using a space ad illustration on a billboard and found to our astonishment that it looked like nothing we had ever seen before. The outdoor advertising agency will provide your artist with a template of the size required for the particular board. The agency usually will also provide artwork and production of the posters themselves. Incidentally, the viewing material that the outdoor advertising agency will provide includes a map of where your group of boards are located.

Most metropolitan areas have agents who handle transit ads, which are nothing more than small billboards used in buses, streetcars, and taxis. When such space is available, it can prove very beneficial, particularly for short-term, local-area promotion.

We have covered only surfaces in this chapter. And, since the entire world of electronic media, as well as all media, is changing even as we write, it will pay you to read more in-depth material on all communications channels including radio, TV, telemarketing, and outdoor advertising.

9

Trade Shows

Trade exhibitions (shows) provide a unique opportunity to make sales presentations directly to prime prospects as well as to dealers, rep organizations, and other market segments where you wish to raise the level of awareness for your company or impress a particular buying influence. A trade show should be planned to tie in with the other elements of your promotional program and should be a showcase from which your salespeople can operate and entice prospects into a one-on-one situation.

Trade shows are an important and effective way of gaining access to individuals and firms who may otherwise be unavailable for a demonstration of your products and services. This medium offers you the chance to have customers come to you rather than your having to make the effort to go to your customers.

Whether it be a fair, exhibition, exposition, industrial or consumer product trade show, seminar or symposium, this type of promotional presentation can be a most cost-effective method of making connections with your target markets.

EVALUATE SHOW BENEFITS

As the communications manager, it is up to you to consider *all* the possible benefits that may accrue from your firm's participation in a particular show. Although the main consideration is, most often, simply the opportunity to generate sales, there are other factors that you should contemplate before ruling a show out on the basis of the lack of high potential sales' generation alone.

TRADE SHOW EVALUATION FACTORS

The following outline describes various areas that should be taken into account when considering a particular trade show.

1. COMPANY NAME IDENTIFICATION
   A. Visibility: To obtain maximum exposure in order to build your firm's desired image as an authority in its market area.
   B. Staying Power: Continued participation in trade shows identifies your firm as having the resources and financial stability essential to a contender in its industry.

2. CONTACT WITH POTENTIAL BUYERS
   A. Purchase Influences: Presents an opportunity to reach a large audience of influences and decision makers (prospective buyers, sales reps, distributors, dealers) who are in a relaxed environment and are willing to spend time discussing your products or services.
   B. Sales Materials: Ability to distribute sales materials directly to potential buyers.
   C. Sales Leads: Opportunity to obtain sales leads

that can be contacted after the show. The level of interest from potential buyers can be measured. Contacts not presently included in the target audience may be identified, resulting in new market exploration.

3. **MEDIA EXPOSURE**
   A. Editorial Contacts: Opportunity to attract editors' attention for meaningful editorial commentary on new or existing product lines.
   B. Promotion: Opportunity to obtain publicity on new product announcements and general press releases.

4. **TRADE SHOW EFFECTIVENESS**
                            Postparticipation evaluation enables you to measure the effectiveness of attending trade shows (effect on sales, name recognition, distributor support), giving further justification for attendance at future shows.

5. **COMPETITIVE AWARENESS**
   A. Information: Opportunity to acquire pertinent competitive information, including:
                            Advertising & marketing information
                            Strategic positioning
                            New product introductions
                            Information that can help your firm differentiate itself and remain a competitive contender in this marketplace.
   B. Competitive Stance: Enables you to keep in stride with competitors who are attending

and using trade shows to successfully increase their contact base
and as a showcase to market their
new products.

IMPACT OF TRADE SHOWS

Trade show organizations provide some general observations regarding
evaluation survey:

- On average, up to 75 percent of attendees at a given trade show
  recall visiting particular booths when questioned as long as four-
  teen weeks after the show.

- As many as 83 percent of visitors with buying influence have not
  been seen by a salesperson from the exhibitor in the preceding
  twelve months.

- It is not unusual for up to 69 percent of attendees to purchase
  within eleven months of the show and for eighty-one percent of
  attendees to purchase within two years.

- On average, 94 percent will report that they found the show to be
  "useful."

GENERAL PROFILE OF THE AVERAGE COMMERCIAL
TRADE SHOW ATTENDEE

Trade show groups also provide some insight about those who attend
trade shows. Up to 75 percent of all attendees at trade shows are buying
influences for at least one of the major product or service categories
exhibited. (*Buying influence* is defined as one who has the final say,
specifies, or recommends.) About 58 percent of the audience did not
attend that same show the previous year and 62 percent attend only one
show per year. It is estimated that 64 percent travel more than 200 miles

to attend a given show and 53 percent spend an average of seven-plus hours on the exhibition floor, speaking with an average of seventeen exhibitors.

IMPORTANCE OF TRADE SHOWS

Trade show participation is especially important if you are involved in the introduction of a new product or the updating of an older one. In order to help you evaluate the potential of a given show, make sure to study the materials provided by the producers of the given exposition in which you are interested. In addition, it would be beneficial to discuss the pros and cons of exhibiting at a trade show with other managers who have been a part of that particular show in past years.

Most likely, you will find that some ad managers will be extremely enthusiastic and maintain that no other medium can provide so many benefits at such a low cost and in such a short time. You may get a less enthusiastic response from others, but most who continue to exhibit will be able to point to specific results and definite advantages gained from exhibiting at shows. However, when a marketing or communications manager has given up on a particular trade show and is working in a market area similar to your own, believe that person when he or she says it was a waste of time and money and not worth the tremendous effort required due to the lack of return. The point is that you should examine and evaluate trade shows very carefully since they are costly and time-consuming operations.

It may interest you to know that approximately four billion dollars a year is invested by industry in trade shows. Budgets for trade shows are exceeded only by newspapers and TV expenditures.

Despite this enormous and growing trade show media, it is probably the least understood of all the promotional avenues we have discussed. In fact, you will be hard pressed to find any course on trade show marketing in any business school.

In addition to the cost of floor space, which varies from show to show, such cost items as the booth itself, carpeting, lighting, equipment, personnel, and advance and postpromotional costs result in a major expenditure, especially when personnel time and expenses are included.

It takes a lot of sales to make any given show cost-effective. Yet, in most instances, we have found that paybacks in qualified leads, company image, and even at-show sales usually justify participation in a given show. This is more likely if the show or conference is carefully selected, thoroughly prepared for, and solid follow up is made.

In addition to national trade exhibitions, you may also find local trade conferences and seminars, which are easy to justify and are far less costly. You also may wish to conduct your own self-supported seminar where you will have complete control of the entire operation.

Whatever route you may take, but most especially in the national show arena, you must devote considerable time and attention to the overall planning, scheduling, and checking. Success at any exhibition will depend on your attention to detail. Small items, such as invitations, hotel reservations, availability of promotional material, demonstration equipment in the booth, audio-visuals, and a list of seemingly insignificant details, if left unattended, can snatch defeat right out of the very jaws of a successful trade show.

Remember—shows can and should be successful, but it takes planning and attention to details in order to achieve this success. If you are unaware of the various shows available to your kind of product or service, we recommend the purchase of the *Official Meeting Facilities Guide,* published by Ziff-Davis, which lists meeting accommodations, equipment, and services available at the facilities throughout the United States and Canada.

We have included a series of trade show information forms in order that you may have a quick guide on developing your own fast-reference material for your particular exhibit.

The first and perhaps most important of these forms is the Basic Show Fact Sheet, which is a summary of critical information you should have at your fingertips. After you have filled in the form, perhaps you will want to send copies to all concerned with the given exhibition in order to have every one tuned in. In addition, we have compiled additional Show Data Forms to assure that every contingency will be considered and that no show requirement will be neglected or forgotten.

◀━━━

Sample: Trade Show Form #1—Basic Fact Sheet

Show Name: _____

Dates: _____

Location: City _____   Hall _____

Booth No.(s): _____

Set-up Dates and Times: _____

1. Show producer: _____

2. Exhibit manager: _____
   Address: _____

3. General-product/service areas covered: _____

4. Attendance: Previous year: _____   Expected this year: _____

5. No of exhibitors: Previous year: _____
   Expected this year: _____

6. Admission: _____   General public _____
   Restricted to trade _____   Restricted to members _____
   Admission price: Public $ _____   Trade $ _____
   Member $ _____   Free _____

7. Data on prior-year participation (if applicable): _____
   _____

8. Participation by competitors: Prior years _____
   _____
   Anticipated competition this year: _____

9. Special reasons for participating this year: _____
   _____

10. Objectives: _____
    _____

Sample: Trade Show Form #2 — Confirmations and Reservations

1. Show Manual Kit received: (date) _____   Booth contract
   returned: (date) _____

2. Booth choices (in order of preferences): _____

3. Both no.(s) assigned: _____   Booth dimensions: _____

4. Deposit of $ _____   Paid on: _____   Balance of $ _____
   Due: _____   Paid: _____

5. Exhibition area obstructions and limitations (if applicable):
   Ceiling height or maximum overhead clearance: _____

Maximum floor loading: _____

Freight elevator dimensions: _____ Capacity: _____ lbs.

6. Exhibit restrictions:
Maximum height of back wall: _____

Maximum height of equipment: _____

Other applicable rules or restrictions: _____

_____

7. Equipment and services needed: (Fill out manual forms)

____ Signs	____ Tables	____ Cleaning service
____ Carpeting/tile	____ Chairs	____ Photographer
____ Flowers	____ Ashtrays	____ Carpenters
____ Telephone	____ Wastebaskets	____ Electrician
____ Spotlights	____ Desk	____ Draperyhanger
____ Electrical service	____ Other	____ Riggers

(If running your own seminar be sure to double check the following list and make sure that any items you need will be made available by the hotel or facility.)

- Coffee for registration
- Coffee and cola for break
- Bar and bartender for cocktail hour
- Stage or platform 1½ to 2 '
- High podium
- Tables for registration, literature, and refreshments
- Electrical extension cords
- 35mm projector and screen
- Remote control with extension cord for projector (have an extra bulb)
- Overhead projector (if needed)
- Microphone
- Table for projector

8. Advance tickets ordered for key customers/others: _____

_____

9. Advance registration and exhibitors' badges ordered for: _____

_____

10. Entertainment suite reserved at: _____
Dates: _____ Suite name/number: _____

11. Hotel reservations made at: _____
for the following:

_____ (Name)   (Date) _____

Sample: Trade Show Form #3—Display Preparation

1. Current Exhibit Booth
   Stored at: _____
   Refurbishing necessary: _____
   Alterations, display copy changes, etc.: _____
   _____

2. Construction of New Booth
   Exhibit builder selected: _____
   Contract approved: _____
   Builder to provide: Model _____   Drawing _____
   Plans _____
   Final design O.K.'d on: _____
   Final sign and display copy, transparencies, photos, samples for
   mounting, etc., due on: _____
   Pre-show set-up and inspection on: _____ At: _____
   _____

3. Exhibit Background
   Products to be highlighted: _____
   _____
   Other products or equipment to be shown: _____
   _____
   Central booth theme: _____
   Principal focal point or attractions(s): _____
   _____
   Special effects to be used: _____
   _____
   Give-away item(s): _____
   Special signs, displays, equipment for entertainment suite: _____
   _____

4. Booth/Suite Personnel (including models)
   Special identification (clothing, name tags, etc.): _____
   Pre-show briefing or instructions: _____
   _____

Sample: Trade Show Form #4—Public Relations: Publicity and Promotions

1. Pre-Show Promotion

Internal promotion (memos, sales letters, etc., to salespeople, reps, others concerned): _____

_____

Booth/suite invitations to customers: _____

Promotional mailing(s) to prospects: _____

(*Note:* A phone call follow-up invitation just before the show is one of the key elements to success)

Other pre-show promotion activities: _____

Pressure-sensitive labels, stickers, or rubber stamp for pre-show correspondence: _____

_____

Postage meter slug: _____

Show tickets/registration forms mailed to prospects or distributed by salespeople: _____

_____

PR information to show management (if requested): _____

2. Show Tie-in Advertising/Promotion

Product releases on: _____

_____ distributed to key industry publications.

Advertising scheduled for special show issues: _____

Press conferences preceding or during show: _____

Other Tie-in Promotions

Advertising in show program: _____

Imprinted give-away literature bags: _____

Imprinted napkins at exhibit refreshment stands: _____

Local signs, billboards, taxis: _____

Special breakfast, luncheon, or cocktail party: _____

Free transportation from airport, or between hotels and convention hall: _____

3. Booth Promotion

Literature to be available in booth for:

General handout: _____

Selective handout: _____

Booth reference only: _____

Inquiry handling: _____

Identification/imprint system: _____

Company inquiry/literature request card: _____

4. Post-Show Promotion

Literature requesting/inquiry fulfillment program: _____

Follow-up mailings: _____

Merchandising of results (in-company house organ, employee newsletter, press, etc.): _____

Sample: Trade Show Form #5 — Transportation and Booth Set-Up

1. Complete shipping address and markings for crates and exhibit materials:

   _____

2. Shipping data: Booth   Products/Equipment
   Shipping date _____
   Shipped from _____
   Via _____
   Routing _____
   Number of pieces _____
   Waybill/Bill of Lading _____
   To arrive on or before _____
   Carrier's office or contact at destination: _____

   _____

3. Official show carrier/drayman: _____

4. Scheduled set up times: _____

   _____

5. Booth erection and dismantling to be handled by:
   _____ Company personnel (list) _____
   _____ On-site labor _____
   _____ Independent exhibit service _____
   Address _____ Phone _____

6. Union situation at exhibit hall: _____

7. Display insurance written or confirmed: _____

Sample: Trade Show Form #6 — After-Show Details

1. Booth dismantling supervision by: _____

2. Disposition of display *products:* _____

_____

Shipping address: _____
Carrier: _____

3. Disposition of *booth:* _____

_____

Shipping address: _____
Carrier: _____

4. Date of shipments: _____
Waybill or Bill of Lading number: _____

5. Hotel and service bills checked and paid: _____

_____

Sample: Trade Show Form #7 — Show Evaluation

1. Total show attendance: _____

2. Quality of attendance from sales standpoint: _____

3. Total estimated booth attendance: _____

4. Number of inquiries/literature requests received: _____

5. Orders and prime sales leads developed during show: _____

6. Reactions to display, general interest level, comments received,
etc.: _____

7. Booth location: Excellent _____ Good _____
Fair _____ Poor _____
Comments: _____

8. Notes on competitor's exhibits, new products, etc.: _____

_____

9. Show management evaluation
Pre-show planning and communications: _____
Adequate services and labor available: _____
Adequate exhibit vs. meeting time: _____
Security arrangements: _____

10. Exhibit hall evaluation: _____
Lighting: _____

Heat/air conditioning: _____

Traffic flow: _____

Fire safety precautions: _____

Transportation to and from hall: _____

11. Cost summary—Exhibit space: _____

                      Services: _____

                      Other display costs: _____

                      Model fees: _____

                      Set-up and dismantling labor: _____

                      Shipping and drayage costs: _____

                      Entertainment suite: _____

                      Hotel and transportation: _____

                      Miscellaneous: _____

                                TOTAL   _____

12. Overall critique of results: _____

    _____

13. Recommendations for future participation: _____

    _____

By: _____ Date: _____

————————————————————————————————▶

SETTING UP SHOW GOALS AND POSTSHOW EVALUATION

Preshow activity should start with a review of your corporate marketing objectives, and progress toward specific goals and strategy for the selected show/audience. Your show objectives should be measurable goals (i.e., generating 300 qualified leads, booking $200,000 in business, demonstrating your new line to 75 percent of the attendees, etc.).

In order to evaluate a show correctly, you should first set up objectives and determine how well they can be satisfied by the particular trade exhibit. For example, the trade show management may be able to supply the answers to such questions as how many attendees at the trade show will be potential customers and prospects. All trade shows are measured on an audit that verifies the number of attendees and a survey that provides an audience profile. Even before you seriously consider exhibiting at the show, you will need to find out the number of attendees interested in seeing your products and the number of attendees who are prospective buyers for your types of products.

These facts can help you determine which products to exhibit, who should staff the booth, how much space to take, how often to demonstrate, and how to plan your preshow promotions.

We have found that the most important element in making your trade show involvement a success is your determination to start planning far enough in advance of the actual show date.

As soon as you decide to participate in a particular trade show, you should write to the exhibit producers and obtain a complete media package on the exhibit. (See Fig. 9-1). This package will usually contain

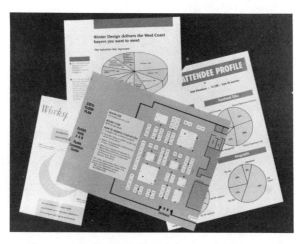

Figure 9-1.   Exhibitor manual material.

a floor plan of the exhibit plus a list of contracts. With manual in hand, you may start to do your overall thinking, which should include:

- Select the particular area you wish your booth to be placed (near a washroom or food concession is usually good).

- Start thinking about the message or theme you want to establish at the booth.

- Establish a realistic budget suited to the theme and display requirements and make a careful selection of booth personnel.

- Make a very tight schedule of the people who will appear in the booth and be certain that they will be there during the appointed hours. The best show or seminar will be doomed to failure if it is not properly staffed. Be sure to take into consideration company personnel changes. There is nothing more disruptive than to have a key person either leave the company or be unavailable to perform as planned at the trade show.

- Make proper hotel reservations.

As you go along, check, again and again, to make sure all show regulations have been met and that your plans are consistent with established show rules.

As the deadline for the show approaches, you will want to review and check inventories of company literature, brochures, data sheets, flyers, and any other printed material you want to have available at the show in order to be sure of having a sufficient quantity of current materials.

Speaking of literature, we have found that it is best not to display and distribute product literature in a serve-yourself fashion. This is wasteful in two ways: First, expensive literature ends up in the hands of the casually interested or "literature collector" and usually ends up being thrown away. Second, the literature is not used in the manner for which it is intended at shows, which is as a screening and classifying device to determine the degree and area of prospect interest.

One of the most expensive items in your trade show budget is printed product literature. We have never been able to understand why companies (especially consumer-product companies) bring so much expensive promotional literature (full-color brochures, catalogs, etc.) for mass dissemination at a trade show.

Our suggestion is to develop a "mini-brochure or back-up catalog," which can be printed in black and white and consist only of an outline of your company's complete product line. These less expensive pieces can be picked up by all the catalog collectors, students, and others who may only be marginally interested in your products (if at all) and the major promotional pieces can be saved for qualified prospects.

This will not only cut down on the waste of your literature at the trade show but it will also make sure that all visitors of your exhibit leave with at least an outline promotional piece that describes all of your product lines. This mini-promotional piece can list all the other catalogs, data sheets, flyers, brochures, and so on that the prospect may obtain by returning an included postage-paid reply card.

This reply card, by the way, can be keyed to the appropriate show and be a source of additional information. It may also include boxes for the prospect to indicate specific areas of interest and whether or not he or she desires a sales call.

Of course, a visitor who openly demonstrates a real need for additional information at the show should be put on a separate inquiry form for immediate response with appropriate product literature.

In addition to making sure your inventory of literature is in good supply, you should also check for any other equipment and supplies. Most particularly, if you are involved in equipment demonstration, make sure your field service people are in attendance and that all equipment is up and functioning properly during the entire show.

A couple of months before the show, you should review all materials provided by show management. Make sure you have submitted all requested forms and contracts, and make arrangements for shipment of product literature and display and exhibit materials in accordance with the show requirements. This is also the time to organize a plan for stimulating attendance at your company's booth and prepare a program of news releases.

Thirty days before you are ready to go to the show, have your display erected at your company or display house and be certain that all bugs are eliminated. Insure your exhibit. Confirm hotel reservations and finalize your booth schedule (advise personnel of their times and what will be expected of them in the booth). Be sure to tell those who are going to be manning the booth that they will be asked for a written report on reactions to the show, sales, and their suggestions for ways to improve the effectiveness of future shows and seminars. Make a final check on shipping arrangements, supplies, literature, products, and hospitality facilities.

Plan to bring your booth to the exhibit hall on the first day your space is available. Set it up as soon as possible in the exhibit hall and have everything ready as far ahead of actual show time as possible.

DIRECTIONS TO BOOTH

One of the most important efforts you can undertake with regard to show participation is the promotion of your booth's location. Most show producers make a variety of devices available to you to assure that you get as many of your prospects to your display as possible. These devices include the distribution of complementary show tickets, which can be imprinted with your company name and booth number. You can send these free show passes to your list of prospects with a letter of invitation.

In addition, show management usually makes available a show logo into which you can incorporate your booth number prominently. You can display this show logo in your space ads around the time of the show. Other devices, such as contests and gifts offered to prospects just for showing up at your display booth, can also generate attendance at your booth. It is extremely important that you do extensive promoting to encourage prospects and customers to come to your booth.

Devices as simple as advertising specialties, candy, or other types of handouts in the aisle can, and should, be used to entice traffic into your booth. Finally, the show producers usually print a program and/ or a show publication in which they make space available to advertisers for a fee similar to regular space advertising. These ads, especially if included in the show program near a booth location map, can be very helpful. But, watch out—they must be carefully evaluated in terms of cost and type of publication (some may be only flyers not connected with the show at all).

HOSPITALITY SUITES

The use of hospitality suites is something that communications managers must evaluate and decide on the basis of individual circumstance and instinct. Our experience has been that it depends mostly on the type of product and sales force. If the salespeople feel it will make an important difference, then go with it—even on a "try anything once" basis.

IN-SHOW SURVEYS

The following is a questionnaire that we used for both a software client and the producers of the trade show itself. It not only attempts to get an overall reading on the show's value but also sounds out the prospects on the software product that was demonstrated in a particular booth. This kind of information can be invaluable, both in show selection and improving performance at the exhibit.

◀───

Sample: Evaluation

Interviewer: _____   Date: _____

Time: _____ A.M.   _____ P.M.   Qstnr #: _____

Section 1.
GOOD MORNING, MAY I TAKE TWO MINUTES OF YOUR TIME? FIRST, I WOULD LIKE TO ASK SOME QUESTIONS REGARDING YOUR VISIT TO THIS SHOW, IN GENERAL.

1. At what time did you arrive at the show today? _____

2. Approximately how many of the exhibits did you walk past? (Read list, check only one)
   All _____
   Most _____
   Half _____
   Less than half _____

3. Approximately how many exhibitors did you talk to about their products or services? _____

4. On a scale of 1 to 10, how informative was this show overall in terms of products and services available for the System/38?
   Uninformative   informative
   1   2   3   4   5   6   7   8   9   10

5. Which exhibitor's product or service stands out in your mind?
   _____
   Why? _____

Section 2.
ONE EXHIBITOR AT THIS SHOW IS ADAROC—WITH THE SOFTWARE PRODUCT "RAMSES." THE FOLLOWING QUESTIONS DEAL WITH THEIR EXHIBIT.

6. Did you pass ADAROC's booth?
   YES   NO (If no, go to Section 3)

7. Did you enter ADAROC's booth?
   YES   NO (If no, go to Section 3)

8. Did you talk with any of the persons in the ADAROC booth about the company's product?
   YES   NO (If no, go to Section 3)

9. Did you sign up to receive the free 30-day demonstration of RAMSES?
   YES   NO

10. Based on materials in the booth or conversations with the AD-AROC people, on a scale of 1 to 10, what is your general impression of the RAMSES software compared with similar types of software with which you are familiar?

    Unimpressed   Very Impressed
    1   2   3   4   5   6   7   8   9   10

11. How likely is it that you or the organization that you represent will give consideration to obtaining the RAMSES software?
    Very likely _____
    Likely _____
    Unlikely _____
    Very unlikely _____
    No opinion _____

Section 3.
NOW, I WOULD LIKE TO FINISH OUR INTERVIEW WITH JUST A FEW QUESTIONS ABOUT YOU AND THE FIRM YOU REPRESENT.

12. In what city and state is your firm located?
    City _____ State _____

13. What is your job title? _____

14. Are you involved in purchase decisions regarding computer products and services?
    YES   NO

THIS INTERVIEW IS NOW COMPLETED. THANK YOU FOR
YOUR COOPERATION.

--➤

STAFFING THE BOOTH

We are firm believers in the use of a specific dress code for everyone
on duty in the booth. We have seen a semi-uniform-type appearance
work wonders, not only for the overall professional look within the
booth but also for the improved attitudes and morale of those tending
the booth. One client changed the booth effectiveness 100 percent simply by having those working in the booth dress in blue blazers with the
company logo embroidered on the front worn with gray slacks or skirts.
This not only produced a better "show look" within the booth, but it
also made a positive impression wherever these employees went
throughout the exhibit hall.

The corporate booth is your business office during the show. Keep
it clean, neat, and professional. The same applies to the staff. The
salespeople who keep late hours, drink heavily, and eat poorly are easy
to spot (and avoid) on the floor. They are the ones with bloodshot eyes
who yawn all day and quietly sit in the corner.

SALES STAFF

Select your sales team early and wisely. For heaven's sake, do not make
the granddaddy of all trade show mistakes by selecting the new recruit
to work the show as a training exercise.

The Trade Show Bureau confirms that 29 percent of the attendees
at trade shows are top management (owners, partners, presidents, vice-
presidents, general managers). Another 51 percent fall into the middle-
management classification. Using novice salespeople for trade show
duty can be suicide for your product and corporate credibility.

OUTSIDE ASSISTANCE

Resource and reference material to aid in the training process for trade shows is very limited. Advertising and marketing courses devote little time to the subject, if they cover it at all. Your best, and sometimes only, alternative is to seek the aid of an experienced exhibit manager for help and advice. If you can find a manager or exhibit house that consistently produces effective shows, ask them to share their knowledge with you. Be prepared to compensate these professionals for their expertise. Their advice and counsel can generate great dividends for you and your company.

In any event, be sure that you provide as much training as possible for those who will be working the booth—even if it is only to let them know what will be expected of them during the hours when they are on duty.

Staff training is not the end-all solution to exhibition success. As with any major undertaking, it takes balance: the right combination of audience, graphics, promotion, exhibit floor location, marketing staff, and training, to name a few areas. However, your staff is the only common denominator that influences the success of all of these elements. Unfortunately, as we indicated, staff training is the weakest link in many faltering exhibit programs. Train your staff and make sure they know that they will be carefully monitored during the show. Our suggestion is to set a system for booth personnel to maintain and follow through, with a report showing how each person working the booth stacked up.

If you are contemplating regular trade show participation, it will be helpful to become acquainted with the Trade Show Association mentioned previously. Also, a subscription to *Trade Show Week* might be a good investment.

The last few years have seen the development of a few publications that you may find helpful with your trade show ventures. In our opinion, two of the best are:

Slide Program:
  "Trade Shows: Successful Sales Techniques"
  Creative Media Development, Inc.
  710 S.W. 9th Avenue
  Portland, Oregon 97205
  (503) 223-6794

Book:
Creative Selling Through Trade Shows
by Hal Hanlon
Hawthorn Books, Inc.
260 Madison Avenue
New York, New York 10016

10

The Creative Effort

As a launching point for our trip into the constantly circulating cosmos of creative communications (nothing like stepping off with a little alliteration), let's take a look at what one famous ad-writing pro says about the art of creative writing. In the book titled *The Art of Writing Advertising,* David Ogilvy is quoted as saying, "I've done as many as nineteen drafts of a single piece of copy. I've written thirty-seven headlines for one ad and when I was done I had three good enough to submit." Keep in mind that Ogilvy has been in the business for many years and has written millions of words of copy. He must still write, rewrite, and continue to rewrite—that's the way good ads are made. This sums up the main method of writing advertising copy, whether it be industrial or consumer. The art of being a good writer is fundamentally to write a lot and select only the best of what you have written.

If some of the following material looks familiar, it is. We have touched on basic writing skills in Chapter 1, looked at writing promotional literature in Chapter 4, and now we are back to our favorite subject once again—creative copywriting.

The point is, nothing important happens in promotional communications until something is put down on paper.

GET THE CONCEPT FIRST

Another extremely important point that we received from an experienced professional copywriter is, "Be sure you understand the concept well before you try to commit words to paper." As this very talented writer said, "You have no trouble speaking and conversing about a subject because you usually have an idea of what you are trying to communicate before, or as you begin, to talk." The same thing applies to writing. When you start to outline your thoughts, be sure that you have your ideas clearly and firmly in your mind and that you understand all the nuances and ramifications.

This means you first must read, research, and think. In other words, put something in before you try to get something out and attempt finished copy.

Once you have the concept, even roughly, in mind, the words will usually flow easily enough, just as they do in conversation. If the idea is reasonably clear, the words will follow. If not, you cannot even start effective copy. After the concept and initial draft, comes the work of polishing as you sit down to edit and re-edit for clarity and impact.

Another great copywriter, William Burnbach, when asked if there was any equation or formula for being a better writer of advertising or what a writer of advertising could do to improve his or her skills, replied, "Well, I wish I could give you an equation so that all you would have to do is follow it, but I can't. What you have to do is keep working, keep thinking, keep being as honest as you can about what you are doing and keep practicing." The message becomes clear: Write, write, and write some more. Keep practicing and trying new approaches is the most important advice anyone can give to the new writer starting in advertising or any field of communications, for that matter.

Incidentally, you will notice that we have selected two major consumer advertising writers to illustrate copywriting points. We did so deliberately in order to emphasize the fact that many times an industrial or technical advertising writer can get some powerful insights and some solid, high-impact ideas from watching and reading the ads directed at the consumer market. This is not to imply that industrial copywriters should plagiarize consumer campaigns, but they can sometimes use the thinking and, oftentimes, an idea or approach.

We have indicated more specifics on creating individual promotional pieces as they have been discussed under various individual promotional avenues. Suffice it to say that there are as many books on writing and writers' tips available to you, both within and without the world of advertising, as you could hope for. Read as many as possible as often as possible. Let's take a look at some simple rules of thumb that will hold you in good stead as you develop more sophisticated approaches and expand your own style when creating effective advertisements and promotional pieces.

Here is a device that you can use in a step-by-step construction of any ad or promotional piece you are about to undertake. The following letters comprise a formula: *A I D C A*. They stand for the words Attention, Interest, Desire, Conviction, and Action.

ATTENTION

In working up any piece of promotion, you must strive for immediate impact in order to gain attention. If you don't catch the eye, all is lost. And again, let's take a quote from a great writer of consumer advertising, Leo Burnett, who said, "If you don't get noticed, you don't have anything. You just have to be noticed, but the art is in getting noticed naturally, without screaming or without tricks."

Notice that this famous writer advises against trickery for its own sake just to gain attention. There are all kinds of attention-getting devices (sometimes called *grabbers*) used in most every type of promotion. Among the most common of these are those hard-hitting headlines you see in bold, dramatic type. Words frequently featured in this type are *FREE, NOW,* and *NEW*. They are still among the most provocative words in the English language even though they were probably used by the world's first copywriter.

The use of the word *YOU* or *YOURS* has also proven to be most effective. After all, the word *you* addresses the reader's most important individual—himself or herself. To check the universal use of *you,* merely flip through the ads in any national publication. Chances are that a good percentage of all the half-page or larger ads will carry that word in the headline or subhead. With over 100,000 words at the copywriter's disposal, *you* is truly a champion.

An appealing illustration, high-impact photo, or other art devices are additional ways of capturing the eye or arresting the attention of the viewer immediately. When we speak of "grabber" headlines, it is important to remember that a purchasing agent or other buying influence in the industrial marketplace can be excited by a headline as mundane as "Now you can reduce costs and cut down time. . . ."

INTEREST

After you have caught the prospect's attention, the next step is to arouse his or her interest. Make no mistake—getting a prospect's interest is equally as important as gaining initial attention.

The futility of gaining attention without acquiring follow-through interest is demonstrated in an ad campaign that ran many years ago for an electronic parts supplier and that appeared in many prestigious publications. The campaign consisted of a fractional space ad (less than a full page) that featured a small pin-up type photo about the size of a postage stamp in the upper left-hand corner. A caption under the photo read something like "Ah-ha, got your attention. Hey! Well, now read all about our marvelous electronic widgets. . . ."

This attention-getting device was followed by some very straight technical copy on semiconductors, or whatever, and for a while, it generated some talk and good humor for the company. The effectiveness of this approach wore thin very quickly, however, and the campaign was eventually dropped, but not before many imitators got into the act with overly cute, meaningless attempts to use an attention getter simply for its own sake.

Approaches such as an upside down ad, an ad placed on its side, pyramid-shaped copy, or unconventional artwork may seem like great attention getters, but if they lack follow-through and fail to arouse interest then they are bound to be ineffective.

These same "gimmick" approaches are just as fruitless when used in brochures, flyers, and other promotional pieces. By the way, we use the term *promotional piece* throughout to include all types of printed materials such as brochures, direct mail letters, flyers, displays, and anything that is produced to carry your promotional message to prospects and customers. Printed promotional pieces are also referred to as *collateral* materials—a buzzword used in advertising agencies to include just about anything that backs up, or is used in conjunction with, mass-media advertising.

Remember, poor advertising can alienate, just as good advertising can attract and persuade. One of the fastest ways to alienate prospects is to produce promotions that dangle promises but do not fulfill initial expectations. We've all seen these types of ads—the ones that disappoint by not giving the reader what is implied at the outset. In other words, they do not reward the reader for the time he or she has spent investigating beyond the catchy headline or body copy "lead ins" that offer information to arouse prospect's interest.

Let's now look at some specific methods used to follow up a given headline and gain that most necessary interest with which to hold the prospect and get him or her into the promotional piece or ad. First of all, there is the use of subheadlines. This device has become more and more popular in recent years and is simply an expansion of the benefits implied in the main headline. The size and style of type selected for the subhead is usually less bold and less dominant than the main headline. However, it is designed to stand out more prominently than the body copy that usually follows. The subheadline tries to expand the main headline and summarize the main focal point of the entire ad, and its benefits can thus entice the reader into the body copy.

In addition to the use of subheadlines to move the reader from simple attention to more prolonged active interest, many other devices are available. These include drawings and illustrations that arouse interest and can be used to involve the reader in the promotional piece. Whether it be a subheadline, bold copy lead-in, or art device, the object of the game is to slow the reader down and get him or her involved in the entire message of the ad, brochure, flyer, direct mail piece, or whatever.

After attention is gained and interest is aroused, you must then stimulate a desire for your product or service in the mind of the reader, which is the third step in our formula for building an effective promotional piece.

DESIRE

Stimulating desire is usually the task for the body copy of the ad or promotional piece. Generally, the first paragraph of the body copy must "pay off" the promises made by the headline and, if one is used, the subheading. Body copy will be discussed further on the next page.

CONVICTION

Let's move back to the overall construction of a promotional piece and get to the fourth part of our formula, Conviction. Conviction can be established in a variety of ways. The most prevalent means of acquiring conviction (or confidence) in your message for the product or service is by a guarantee or warranty. This is the most direct approach and the most effective one as well. Another effective method is the use of testimonials that provide the reader with the ability to identify with someone who has already used the product or service successfully. Testimonials, warranties, and guarantees are effective in gaining the conviction you are looking for in your promotional message.

ACTION

Action is what is commonly known as the "bottom line." It is often what separates the pros from the amateurs—simply asking your reader to take some kind of action. It is so disappointing to see a good promotional piece dressed up in exquisite artwork and magnificently printed on expensive stock go down the drain simply because the creator did not request—even better, demand—action from the audience. As important as this is, it is the most forgotten element in promotional writing.

Forgetting to ask for the order is an unpardonable sin for any good salesperson. Any communicator who does not direct the reader to some action is guilty of the same sin. One of the most reliable and direct ways to move the prospect to action is to use the tried-and-true coupon device. It is estimated that a 10 to 18 percent response can be gained from the use of a coupon in an ad or a post-paid reply card in direct mail.

BODY COPY

We have discussed the writing of body copy and have determined that it is an art unto itself. Good, effective advertising copy comes only after much study and long practice. For now, however, we will give you yet another formula that may be applied to writing copy and will help you as you develop skill and expertise in the writing of promotional copy: *P R E P*.

Let's assume you have a fairly decent headline and a reasonably strong subhead; now you are ready to get to the crux of your message and tell a more complete story in the plotting of your promotional piece. We suggest that as you start, you write the letters *P R E P* and let these stand for the words Point, Reason, Example, and Point again.

POINT

As we have said, good copy should first of all "pay off" the headline; that is, fulfill the promise stated or implied in the headline of the ad or promotional piece. Then, very quickly, within the first paragraph of the copy, the main point, or the case for the product, should be made in a logical step-by-step manner. As the copy continues, it should cite the various benefits provided in the order of their importance to the prospective customer.

Please notice the importance of that last point. It is absolutely critical that before you start writing copy you know the audience to whom you are writing. So many promotions are written without any seeming knowledge of the audience to whom they are directed that it becomes impossible to trace the motivation behind or the thinking put into them.

Advertising agencies, particularly, can be guilty of writing to please a client rather than writing to reach an audience. Copywriters often forget to write to the readers' interest. When you start to write that all-important first paragraph of body copy, try to put yourself into the shoes of the person you are trying to persuade—keep the reader interested.

Not directing the copy to a known audience often results in the "brag and boast" type of ad found in many trade journals. This is also called *flag waving* since, in past days, it was represented by ads that always included a photograph of the company building with the American flag in front and perhaps a photo insert of the corporation's president or founding father. The "brag and boast" approach today comes much better disguised than in the past. Disguised or not, you can pick these ads out by their pompous posture and lack of specific prospect benefits.

Usually such ads and promotional pieces talk about how long the company has been in business, make general proud claims of superiority, and never get down to a specific product benefit or point. Really, now, who cares that your company was founded in 1776 or that your "craftsmen have more ingenuity" than anyone else in the world?

The effective ad will, first of all, take the strongest possible benefit, make a point of it in the first paragraph and make that point in the strongest possible way. Notice, please, that important word *benefit*. What we mean here is a *benefit* to the prospect, not a *feature* of the product. This may seem like a fine point but it is not. We will elaborate later.

There are many appeals that your promotion may choose, ranging from how your product or service saves money, how it costs less than a competitor's product, how it makes the customer's operation more efficient, and so on. Whichever approach or appeal you take, make it strong and make it fast. As the old axiom in advertising states, "Tell me swift and tell me true or else my dear, the hell with you." Get to the major point that you are trying to express to the audience you are trying to reach—fast.

REASON

Now, having made our initial point, we move to the second part in our copywriting acronym, Reason. Following our initial "Point," we need to back up our appeal with a specific reason why you, your product, or your service has this advantage or benefit. Here again, the reason why you can make particular claim will be found within the product itself. For example, if you claim that your product can save the customers time and money, then you must be able to tell them why. The reason could be anything from new state-of-the-art technology to simply a better packaging of your product.

EXAMPLE

The next thought you should try to interject into your body copy is a specific example. You have the lead paragraph making the "Point" that your product saves the customer money. You tell him or her the "Reason" is that you have advanced technology over existing products. You now go to a specific example, preferably a testimonial from someone who has actually used the product and will testify to the advantages you have already stated.

POINT AGAIN

The last phase of the promotional copy should be to point again, or to restate your initial point. To paraphrase an old huckster after-dinner speaker and pitchman, "Tell 'em, then tell 'em what you told 'em. Then, tell 'em again."

Now, just to summarize the basics, we will take a run through a typical promotional piece. Let's say, for example, we want to build an ad for an X-ray envelope. (See Fig. 10-1.)

Figure 10–1. Sample X-Velope ad.

First of all, we sit down and look carefully at the product and find that it is put together with new, technically advanced, plastic bubbles, which provide two immediate benefits. First, the envelope is lighter, and second, it is stronger than competitive products. Let's assume that a name has been coined that will describe the product in terms of its function, and, after a dozen or more names were rejected, the name "X-Velope" was selected.

Let's also assume a logotype was designed that incorporates the name "X-Velope" with the follow-up explanatory words *X-ray film mailing envelope*. Now, some artwork has been put together with the trade name and the follow-up phrase to provide a complete "signature": "X-Velope . . . X-ray film mailing envelope."

Let's next look at our main headline that drives home the most important benefit, that is, the savings in postage costs. Notice that the word *new* and the specific cost savings are included. Also notice that a photo is used in the ad to gain specific interest. We get our *desire* by repeating the cost savings plus other benefits right off in the first paragraph.

The second paragraph gives the *reason:* "Space-age materials." We get our *conviction* from the testimonial implication, "Developed for use in the Radiology Department of Massachusetts' largest teaching hospital."

Last, notice the free offer ("prove it to yourself") and the coupon that makes it easy for the prospect to respond.

GOOD PROMOTIONS GIVE IN ORDER TO GET

Whatever promotional form you may be undertaking, the guidelines presented here can keep your copy on track. Probably the most important rule of all is: Every promotion must give in order to get. Unless your promotion informs, entertains, educates, or somehow provides the reader with a reward for the time he or she spends with your message, your promotion will most probably fail.

Just one other note while we are still on creative basics: Remember, as we stated earlier, you, as a communicator, will be called into all phases of your company's marketing endeavor. It is important that you think not only in terms of making an ad or promotional piece, but also in broader creative terms. Be alert to what your company has to offer or may be missing.

The following will serve as an illustration of this point. A long time ago, we were employed by a major fastener company as ad manager and became interested in the company's past history. Snooping around to find some grist for the promotional mill, we came across a large cabinet, buried deep within the lower regions of the factory area. The cabinet had hundreds of drawers filled with blueprints and samples of various types of fasteners that the company had designed and produced for individual customers over the years. After going through dozens of boxes of items such as rivets used as studs in automobile tires (which were outlawed and have since made a comeback) and the like, we came across a drawer that contained a clip of oversized staples. It was not until we had studied the blueprints and reviewed the correspondence that we realized we were looking at a stapling device developed long before the time of the staple had come.

This fastener company had designed and produced a product for fastening paper which was sold to a single customer and immediately forgotten. Later, this same type of device—the stapler—made its inventor a fortune. Wouldn't you have liked to have been the communicator who picked up on this innovation and promoted its advantages universally?

LAYOUT

Layout, visualization, and artwork play significant roles along with copywriting in the communication of a motivating message.

Too often, in developing an ad or promotional piece, inexperienced individuals will take the various elements that will be used—headline, subhead, body copy photographs, logotype—and place them in the available space with little thought given to an appealing layout. They forget that the objective of the layout is to work with and dramatize the headline.

In most cases, the marketing communicator should rely on an ad agency, an in-house artist, or a free-lance designer to develop the layouts for ads and collateral materials. However, it may be useful to bear in mind a few of the basic elements of good layout.

Good layout features balance. There are two kinds of balance: formal and informal or static and dynamic.

When developing your layout you may want to draw a vertical pencil line that divides the piece into two equal halves. When 50 percent of each element appears on the right and 50 percent on the left of this line, that's true balance, which can be dull. In dynamic balance, half of the material appears on the left and half on the right side of the vertical line but each element does not balance itself. For example, a block of copy might balance a major illustration, or a logotype and trademark might balance a headline and subhead. Each side balances the other visually—it looks right. Figure 10–2 shows a straightforward,

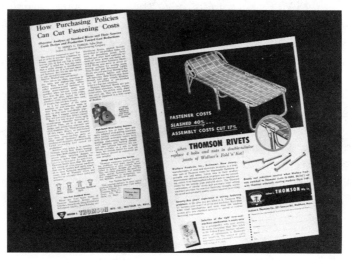

Figure 10–2.   Static and dynamic ads.

heavy copy, static informative ad along with a more dramatic, informal, heavily illustrated ad, both for the same fastener company promoting the same product.

Another principle to keep in mind is the gazer's eye motion. Each element in your ad should lead the casual reader's eye through the ad, from headline to signature, following the path you have predetermined.

Simplicity stands as a must in effective advertising layout. Keep the number of elements in your ad to a minimum. If you have several illustrations that you wish to include, have them overlap so that several isolated, independent elements become one. Don't be afraid to use lavish use of white space if the opportunity presents itself. Many advertisers want to cram every inch of the ad space with copy or illustrations because they are paying for that space. A welcome and judicious use of white space adds immeasurably to the appearance of the ad, inviting readership.

VISUALIZATION

Although most anyone can produce a very rough layout, we normally call on a commercial artist to give us a finished layout. The story of the development of effective visualization differs from this approach. Anyone can come up with the visualization concept for an advertisement—the ad manager, the artist, the marketing director, the switchboard operator, or the little boy who lives down the street. Not many will do a good, or even fair, job at making an ad, brochure, or whatever, but they can all visualize.

What, then, is visualizing? It involves the development of a procedure that enables us to tell a story in pictures rather than in words. Truly creative advertising people can put together a series of exciting ideas for conveying pictorial messages.

Visualization can be the most significant element in the development of an advertisement. When you come up with a blockbuster of an idea for the illustration, it really does not matter whether or not you are a competent artist. You can turn that visual over to the agency, company artist, free lancer, or photographer with whom you may be working and let them flesh out the art. Once again, it is the basic idea that counts.

A few years ago we were friendly with a gentleman working for one of New York City's leading ad agencies. He was one of the highest-paid creative talents in the agency, yet he had some trouble in putting together a series of coherent sentences in a block of copy and he could not draw a straight line with a ruler. However, he could visualize. He came up with many pictorial story approaches that were produced effectively in well-known national campaigns. He simply had the talent to communicate to the copywriters and to the artists the stories that he wanted the advertisements to convey.

There are a number of ways to handle visualizing a problem. The least successful, in most instances, is just to show the product alone. If you are promoting a television set, for example, don't show only the set. At the very least, put it in some sort of setting, like a living room or den (or perhaps a hen house if you feel creative enough to tie in a headline that applies), which will add some interest by way of illustration and provide the grabber you need to capture initial attention.

If no other idea presents itself, a tried-and-true visualizing technique is to show the product in use. Going back to the TV example, featuring it in a den is fine, but human interest becomes a part of the appeal if you have someone watching the screen. If you're selling a drill, show someone using it; if you're selling a car, have someone driving it; if you're promoting dog food, feature Fido busy at his dish.

Other techniques include the depiction of the disadvantage of not using the advertiser's product or, conversely, the advantages of using it. Some companies, both in and out of the industrial markets, have developed trade characters whom they use to tell their stories. In the consumer field, we have outstanding examples such as the Green Giant, Little Lulu, Mother Nature, the lonely washing machine repairman, and a host of others—all good visualizers.

In closing this chapter on communicating creatively to consumer and industrial markets, let's reemphasize the importance of being direct, swift, and penetrating. (See Fig. 10–3.)

Figure 10–3. Various high-impact headlines. (Used with permission of United Technical Products, Inc., 960 Turnpike Rd., Canton, MA 02120.)

Keep in mind the fact that about 85 percent of space ads do not even get noticed and that a reader of any given trade publication may spend as little as six minutes leafing through the entire publication—ignoring your ad completely, if it does not have impact. The same grim reality holds true for direct mail pieces, brochures, and any promotional piece you may produce.

The competition is fierce and only the best get noticed. When constructing your promotion, do not forget A I D C A: Attention, Interest, Desire, Conviction, and Action.

Also remember P R E P for Point, Reason, Example, and Point when you are writing your main body copy. These ideas will help swing the odds in your favor toward those 15 to 20 percent most noted ads in any given publication.

As the communicator for your company, you will be responsible for a considerable amount of your firm's money. Remember, a small, well-created ad with impact and interest, tied together with appropriate publicity and coordinated with a direct mail campaign, can be fortuitously productive. Think, of course, but think *creatively.*

11

Parting Shots

This chapter is our attempt to sum up a few of the more important lessons gleaned from working with and promoting hundreds of products/services for a wide range companies (very small to extremely large).

Perhaps you are now, or shortly will be, in the communications business. If so, you probably know that among your more important efforts will be to gather, distill, and utilize information.

This chapter provides an opportunity to practice your communicator's skills by assimilating some of these observations into the development of your own style and using others as warnings against some ineffective concepts that you may wish to avoid.

Many of the pearls of wisdom cast here can be found buried in case history material scattered throughout various previous chapters. We could not resist a brief recap of a few fundamental bits of knowledge acquired from our promotional work with so many different companies and products.

Pearl #1: Know Your Company . . . Know Your Job . . . Know That It Is All Subject to Change Without Notice

Our first pearl of wisdom comes from understanding and appreciating the many-faceted role played by the manager who undertakes to perform the communications function.

This is a role both authors have played under such titles as Ad Manager, Public Information Officer, Public Relations Manager, Director of Marketing, and others.

Whatever the title, the essence of the job is usually the same: Find out what the corporate goals are and try to achieve them, as much as possible, through the all-important communications function.

This may sound simple and you might expect to find these objectives written in a company business plan or a marketing strategy somewhere. Do not be too surprised if you find that management, rather than providing specifics on its basic direction, gives you a vague and useless mandate like "get in there and increase company sales."

When this happens it is usually because management is in a state of transition and goals and objectives are in the process of being reevaluated. As a matter of fact, this is the usual rather than the unusual case because if the corporation is growing, it is changing. Indeed, your addition to the staff may reflect some of the new directions being undertaken. Understand that they may be looking to you to help in setting new directions and not to steer a dull course back to the past.

Vague objectives do not make your job easy but this kind of situation does provide you with the challenge and opportunity to investigate and get your own understanding of the firm's mission down on paper. This effort, more than any other you can perform, will show that you know where the starting line is and will prove that you are thinking in terms of the overall good of the company.

Once you have some kind of verification from management on what the corporate objectives are and have committed them to paper, you then must get some agreement on priorities. Once objectives are stated and priorities are set, it is time to write a communication program and obtain management agreement and approval.

Make sure that your plan is tied directly to the objectives already presented and reflects the priorities already set and you will have performed a basic and critical service for your firm.

Finally, you move from the agony of detailed preparation to the ecstasy of actually implementing your communications plan. This is where you follow through and make your program work in the most effective, creative, and economical way you can devise, and always with the full knowledge that, even as you are busy breaking your neck getting the job done, all of the priorities, and even the objectives themselves, may be changing due to the ever-shifting policies being set at the top.

We stress this point about change because we feel that it is important that you know that you will be working in a constantly changing environment and that to survive you must be ready to adapt to it.

For example, when the writer first went to work for the fastener company mentioned previously, he was told that his job was to create the "most favorable climate" in which the company could sell its fasteners. Armed with this vague direction, he set forth all kinds of activity such as working with the ad agency creating ads, getting out direct mail, going to trade shows, developing sales support materials, writing newsletters, and more.

Suddenly, one day, that seventy-five-year-old fastener company was bought out by a venture capital organization. The employees were told that everyone's job was secure and that nothing important would really change. (Be sure to add this comment to the list of "check-is-in-the-mail" cliches if you are ever involved in a company takeover.)

When the writer found himself spending most of his time conducting plant tours for visitors from all over the world, it began to dawn on him that his job was no longer promoting the sale of the company's products but, rather, the selling of the company itself.

The new owners had changed direction quickly and completely. Tasks that previously had been considered vital were no longer important and although the previous work was complimented, it was no longer what new management wanted. The writer now had the choice of shifting his efforts or looking for another job. It was unfortunate that many who had been with the firm for many years could not, or would not, change their mind-set and were soon asked to resign or were fired.

As for the writer, he showed such flexibility that he was not only kept on but promoted to director of marketing. So, to recap our Pearl #1, constantly be aware of corporate objectives and management perspectives *and* when priorities change, you change.

Pearl #2: Agency versus Non-Agency

Actually this second pearl of wisdom covers a lot of territory beyond the involvement or noninvolvement of an advertising agency. The ability to know when and how to engage or not to engage a professional outside support group such as an advertising or public relations agency encompasses many levels of judgment and many years of good and bad experiences.

SETTING UP AN IN-HOUSE AGENCY OR AD DEPARTMENT

If yours is a small industrial/technical company and you do not have the budget or the inclination to hire an outside ad agency, you may want to perform the agency function yourself. Be warned, however, even if you own the company and you are its entire staff, that you will need some creative support—printers, writers, artists, photographers, and the like—to assist you in producing effective, successful communications materials. Many managers have started out using free-lance talent and later built it into what is called an *in-house agency* (i.e., an ad agency completely owned and controlled by the advertiser and run by the company manager).

ADVANTAGES OF DO-IT-YOURSELF ADVERTISING

Among the advantages in running an in-house operation are:

1. There is more control over the individuals performing the actual work.
2. There is better and faster understanding of the company and its products.
3. Input on collateral materials needs is more informed.
4. Turnaround and response to market conditions are faster.

Working the agency operation yourself also saves the frustration of educating and reeducating agency people as they come and go through an outside ad agency.

Usually an internal house agency will cost slightly less to operate than an outside operation, particularly if you are set up to obtain media commissions (15 percent discount on space and time costs). However, *do not* base your decision on cost savings alone and especially not on saving the 15 percent agency commission since this factor *alone* will not justify setting up and running such a complex and demanding operation.

One of the most important advantages of going in-house is that you get to work directly with the people doing the job rather than through an account executive. Being fully involved with the creative and production activities will teach you communications skills faster and more efficiently than anything else you can try. Also, the personal rewards that come from building your own creative/production team are indescribable.

DISADVANTAGES OF IN-HOUSE OPERATIONS

The disadvantages of the in-house agency or running the entire communications show on your own include a limited creative capability, the possibility of too much control by management, and the incestuous rehash of ideas without a fresh look at new approaches to your markets. Remember that there are many in-house operations that are the most effective and efficient way that particular firm can get their promotional job accomplished—just as there are companies where not having an ad agency would be tantamount to giving up their communications program altogether.

So, there is really no simple answer to the agency/no agency question (although this book was written more to those who decide to go on their own). It is a tough decision and best answered by communications managers who have solid, realistic ideas of their promotional needs.

WORKING WITH AN AGENCY

If yours is a medium- to large-size company and you *do* have the budget and the inclination to hire an outside ad agency, you will derive some very definite advantages from putting this kind of resource to work for you.

THE ADVERTISING AGENCY: A BRIEF HISTORIC INTERRUPTION

There are many stories on how the advertising agency industry got started but the one that seems to be backed up historically involves a bright young lad who offered to have a church bulletin printed free of charge if the pastor would allow him to place some messages on the back page of the bulletin. When the pastor agreed to this arrangement, the lad was off and running to sell "space" to the local butcher, baker, candlestick maker, and all the town merchants. To the merchants he offered to produce the ad and place it in the bulletin—for a fee. Events marched and before long our bright young lad was making a fine profit and so have his kind ever since.

TYPES OF AGENCIES

Today there are many distinct kinds of ad agencies—consumer, industrial, technical, as well as a range of creative boutiques and specialty agencies that concentrate on a specific industry or even an individual type of product.

We recall one agency that dealt only with firms involved in the shoe industry. We could never understand how this agency resolved the apparent conflict of interest in handling so many competing firms but their clients didn't seem to mind and the firm flourished.

Today's advertising agency performs many functions far beyond the writing and placing of advertisements. Media selection alone has become an independent science. With so many publications reaching so many diverse audiences, it becomes critical that the publication with the most appropriate audience be selected or the message will certainly fall on deaf ears.

One of the primary benefits your agency can provide is working with you on your budget. You should turn to your agency for help before allocating your funds into various promotional channels.

Whatever type or size agency you select, make sure that you inform all the agency players of your overall plan and keep them updated on your changing objectives and policies.

In years past, a 15 percent commission was paid by the publication to the advertising "agent" for his or her labors. At that time, it made little sense not to hire an agency since the client paid 15 percent more than the agent did to place an ad in a publication. In effect, whatever creative and other work the agent performed was at little or no cost to the advertiser since the agent derived income (15 percent discount) from the publication.

This is no longer the situation. Companies with large budgets (TV advertisers, for example) now negotiate different payment plans to reduce extremely large commissions from enormously large budgets. On the other hand, smaller companies with less expansive budgets, and thus smaller commissions available to the agency, require the client to pay a fee to cover the cost of agency services. In addition to the creative help, a prime benefit derived from employing an advertising agency of record (usually a fully accredited outside agency currently handling your account) is the assistance they can provide in planning your overall program—allocating your budget and balancing various campaigns in terms of your marketing strategies and goals.

THE BALANCED PROGRAM

We have found that the most common mistake made by communications managers who decide to perform the ad agency function themselves, is that they may yield to the temptation of doing what they know best to do, what they like to do, or what has worked best for them in the past. Although this is less likely to happen with an outside ad agency, there can be different kinds of problems with some agencies. The most common pitfall here is the agency that advises heavy space commitments because of commissions or just because it is caught up in an overenthusiastic corporate image building effort.

On the other hand, we have known communications managers who, overeager to impress top management with instant results, have put too much emphasis on inquiry-pulling direct mail programs. These "instant" sales leads campaigns, in some cases, have so overwhelmed the overall program and exhausted the budget that other promotional avenues, such as publication advertising and publicity, and their longer-term awareness goals were sacrificed. The program becomes subjective and, rather than building a balanced, cost-effective promotional plan, winds up as a narrow, lopsided effort.

Remember that there are a number of basic promotional avenues available to get to a given marketing destination. These include direct mail, space advertising, trade shows, publicity, public relations, radio, TV, telemarketing, and others. The vehicle or avenue you use should be determined by where you are going or whom you want to reach, how fast you want to reach them, and whether it is a short- or long-term goal you are trying to achieve.

For example, let's say you are going for a short-term ride to reach a specific, well-defined audience that you simply want to influence to purchase your company's new product right away. Since you know your audience, direct mail would probably be most efficient and since immediate sales are the only goal, the message could perhaps be a cost saving or discounted price on your product for a given period.

On the other hand, if you are trying to build prestige and awareness for your firm for the long run and your message is to convey quality and stability, then an image-building space ad in a leading national trade, business, or consumer publication, stressing the company's strength and special capabilities, would be more in order.

Pearl #3: Get to Be a Professional by Listening to Professionals

There is an old axiom you should remember: "Learn to listen and listen to learn." We have been extremely fortunate in our associations with interesting, experienced professionals in all phases of the communications business. From our personal experience, we have found that listening to these professionals is the fastest, surest, and easiest way to acquire all the varied attributes of the successful communications manager.

LESSONS FROM A PRINTER

Perhaps the earliest and most important influence on this author's particular career was a printer named Max, who owned a small print shop in the local area. He did most of the printing for the company where I held my first job in communications as advertising manager. Whenever

I would bring in a job to be printed, Max would walk me through the shop and discuss ways of improving it. We would examine various jobs in process as we reviewed the job I had at hand. He might recommend a heavier stock than I had in mind or perhaps the use of a colored stock for greater impact without the cost of printing a second color. (I still suggest a colored stock in a heavy weight for many black-and-white jobs since it adds so much and costs so little more than a plain white piece of regular lightweight litho stock.)

Whatever suggestions Max made, they inevitably improved the piece. Since that time, I have always consulted the printer in the early stages of every job. In nine cases out of ten, this practice has resulted in a better promotional piece, oftentimes at less cost.

Max also taught lessons in areas other than printing. For example, I remember Max saying that you could always tell a printer by the way he opened his mail. Since printers deal with artwork and small pasted pieces of type, it becomes a habit for them to check the envelope or package very carefully. They will often rip the envelope apart for a final search before it is discarded. This little trick has saved art and type from being lost on more than one occasion.

Over the years, many other production people became my instructors and every job became, and still is, a learning experience. Typesetters, photostat makers, every supplier is a new source of practical, professional help and information.

LESSONS FROM AN ARTIST

"I don't know much about art but I know what I like." This famous cliché is used by people who would like to critique artwork in terms of their subjective feelings. The toughest thing for the artist to face is the client who throws a remark like, "I'm sorry, this piece just doesn't hit me here," pointing to where one's heart should be.

We have found that a good writer and a good artist, given a well-defined objective, can produce good promotional materials. However, a good artist and a good writer, working together over the years as an experienced team, will very often produce a great promotional piece. This writer especially has been most fortunate in working with the same artist on most collateral materials over a number of years. This writer/artist team provides a working relationship that enables both parties to "mind read" each other's direction and, in a relaxed brain-storming session, arrive at a distinctive new approach to practically any promotional project.

This closeness allows a writer to rely on an artist to take his or her words and visualize them with type, line drawings, or photo arrangement designed in a way to produce maximum impact. The artist who generates this kind of confidence provides the writer with clear visual expression of his or her ideas. The artist will teach news ways to look at presenting the theme and objectives of the promotional piece. He or she will also teach sense of proportion, layout and design sense, sense of color, and how to combine all the art elements for maximum effect. By working with the artist, you can not only develop new insights into the presentation of your promotional piece but also new ways of viewing the entire world of art.

LESSONS FROM A WRITER

When entering the communications business, this writer worked first without the benefit of an ad agency. I did, however, have the good sense to hire an oldtimer in the business who was copy chief at a medium-sized agency. His name was Brad. He would freelance in the early evenings or on weekends and he loved to write. His copy was crisp and clear and he was a master at putting down the heart of the message in twenty words or less.

He worked "by the light of the moon," a phrase that he coined for freelancing or moonlighting. Working with this writer was not only a most valuable learning process for me personally but it also produced a great deal of excellent copy. It allowed me to direct my promotional program rather than being bogged down in the writing effort. This experience not only taught me the basics of solid, hard-hitting copywriting but also showed me that all successful promotions start with the writer's concept. Everything—ad campaigns, direct mail programs, even art directions—starts with the writer's creative concept.

LESSONS FROM A PHOTOGRAPHER

I also became close friends with a local commercial photographer, Danny, and, although I never followed photography as I did the writing discipline, I became adequate with a camera and, in a pinch, was able to take some reputable photos for anxious low-budget clients. This experience provided the ability to direct a photographic "shoot" with a professional eye. It also brought an awareness and understanding of such areas as composition, lighting, retouching, and lab techniques. To this day, I keep my hand in this art and am able to take a quick black-and-white product shot, develop and print a glossy in the darkroom, and get it reproduced in quantity (multiprints) for an "emergency" publicity release deadline. This semi-pro capability has saved the day for me (and my clients) on more than one occasion.

INFORMATION FROM SPACE/TIME REPRESENTATIVES

Another valuable source of information and direction is a publication representative (space rep). Along with radio and TV reps (time/sales people), space reps provide valuable knowledge of a particular audience or given market segment, including demographic data, updated trends, and the like. It has been our experience that the most definitive and helpful information comes from trade publication reps, especially those whose magazines are involved with the same general product category in which you are interested. "Trade book" reps, after all, are out in your industry talking to your competitors and working with editors who are writing up-to-the-minute news stories and articles on subjects most important to you and your company. Reps also know what is going on in all the ad agencies and can tell you, better than any other single source, who is doing what and why in your market.

HELP FROM ASSOCIATIONS

Yet another effective way to learn your profession and stay on top of your job is to join associations involved with communications, as well as organizations concerned with the same product or service area as your firm.

You will find that your fellow communicators, even in dissimilar operations, have very similar problems. By sharing various approaches, information on suppliers, trade show effectiveness, promotional campaigns, and the like, you will expand your mind-set and capabilities considerably. Trade associations provide equally important benefits in specific product areas.

Do not hesitate to join an ad club, a marketing club, a PR club, and other professional associations where you can swap ideas and information. Remember that most of your important learning starts after your formal education has been completed.

Pearl #4: When and How to Hire an Advertising Agency

Many people think they should hire an advertising agency as soon as they have enough money. However, a "do-it-yourself" operation or in-house agency is a viable way to go depending on your particular set of circumstances and needs. Since we detailed all the promotional know-how available from suppliers and others sources mentioned above, it may appear that we are leaning toward the "you-do-it" side. This, of course, is partially true. In fact, the main reason for this book is to make you at least somewhat self-sufficient and able to better handle communications tasks yourself. That said, however, we are not suggesting that you do not at least consider utilizing a professional ad agency. As indicated previously, this choice, which you should make carefully, will depend on your own particular situation.

ADVANTAGES OF THE PROFESSIONAL AD AGENCY

One special advantage held by an advertising agency is its ability to attract the most creative people available. An agency can assemble all types of talent—copywriters, artists, marketing specialists, research people, and so on—into an cohesive team which, over time, has or will handle just about any advertising/communications/marketing problem you will ever have to face.

Since the sole purpose for the agency is its ability to promote products, they learn to do it very well or they simply cease to exist. Remember, an ad agency has nothing to sell but time and talent—their prime effort is to provide creative solutions to marketing/communication problems.

An ad agency also thinks in terms of continuing campaigns and total programs as opposed to many corporate management people who tend to think in terms of making a single ad or direct mail piece based on whatever idea springs from a pet concept or sudden instinct.

A good agency will not simply make an ad. It will create a total promotional program derived from solid marketing information and thorough knowledge of the audience they are seeking to influence. Also, the agency will do it so that it affects potential customers in the most dynamic and persuasive way imaginable.

Yet another peripheral plus for an agency is that it often commands management respect simply because it is the outside communication council rather than a "philosopher" within your own company. The agency's ability to shoot down a pet brainstorm from the corporate president with less emotional risk is something to consider. A good agency can serve to back you up as a professional and minimize management meddling as well.

Perhaps the most important benefit you will derive from an ad agency is having the support in all the areas mentioned—planning, writing, art, production, and the like, which will allow you more time to manage. We believe that an agency is there to "do." Your job, as manager, is to concentrate on the reasons why they are doing what they are "doing." With a good agency at your command, you can give directions rather then spend all your time being creative or involved with production details best left to the professional at your agency (or in-house staff, if that is the direction you have taken).

PICKING YOUR PARTICULAR PROMOTIONAL PARTNER

The basic questions to ask when considering a particular advertising agency are how well it will translate the direction you provide into cost-effective promotions and how much it will charge for the assignments you set down for it.

Selecting the right agency is not an easy task and there are a number of rules of thumb that you may use. The overriding consideration is the agency's ability to work with you and become a true member of the company team. As for agency costs, they are usually negotiable and will depend, to a certain degree, on space and time billing and agency income in the way of commissions from these sources. Also, much will depend on the kinds and amounts of service you require. For example, if you intend to perform the publicity function yourself, the agency should be informed that this effort will not be required and, therefore, will not be an income-producing area.

EVALUATING THE AGENCY TEAM

It has been said that picking your agency should be done as carefully as selecting your spouse. The partnership you form with the agency you select will not only determine the direction of your own career, but will also vitally affect the success of your company. First and foremost, it is absolutely critical that you feel confident and comfortable with the people in the agency and know from the start that you will be able to develop a close working relationship with whomever is finally chosen.

This means that when you interview ad agencies you should make sure that the people who are making the presentation include the people with whom you will be actually working. Larger agencies often use new business teams that are extremely expert in making sales presentation and closing accounts. However, they may not be the people with whom you will interface later. Make sure you interview the account people, and even the production, art, and copywriting staff, to see if you feel comfortable with them.

We were once approached by a marketing manager to put together a presentation team that he hoped would help his management pull themselves together and hire a professional group to promote their small commuter airline. Because time was so short and the need so desperate, we had to hire people on a very temporary basis. All this short-term staff had to do was sit in and "role play" functions such as media director, production manager, traffic coordinator, and the like. Of course, we had our permanent agency core group who would be working with the marketing manager and who were sufficient to handle all of the account's requirements. Our effort was to dispel management's feeling that they needed a cast of thousands for which, of course, they would never have been willing or able to pay.

After winning the account, we did actually fill one additional slot but, as you may have guessed, after the presentation no one ever asked again about our staff.

Another instance involved a cosmetic corporation that had the nasty habit of pulling the rug out from an agency every two or three years (just when the agency was acclimated and starting to show some profit). This, they claimed, was in order to obtain constantly new, fresh people on the account. Little did they know that once their account team left the agency, so did many of the creative people, who hopped right over to the new agency providing "fresh new ideas" under the new agency name. So, check the people in the agency you are considering. After all, as we said in an earlier headline, "The people make the difference."

A SURE WAY TO KNOW WHAT AN AGENCY CAN DO FOR YOU

It has always seemed to us that the traditional agency selection process of the speculative presentation is both wasteful and haphazard. It is wasteful for the agency that must put together costly "dog and pony" shows and haphazard for the client who is viewing a series of impromptu approaches that can only be evaluated subjectively.

We believe that the best procedure for hiring an ad agency is to give each applicant a specific assignment and pay the cost set by the agency to do that particular job. This way, you and your company will find out what the agency team can really do, how they interface with you, and get some idea of their cost structure. In addition, you will most likely wind up with several usable promotions rather than a maze of agency proposal materials, none of which can be used except those submitted by the winner.

PICKING YOUR AGENCY BY SIZE

As a general rule of thumb, it is wise to go with an agency where you are about 20 percent of the total billing. If you are among the smaller clients, you are the little fish in the big pond and may not get the attention you require. If you are responsible for more than 20 percent of the agency's billing, you may dominate and perhaps intimidate the agency into pleasing you, rather than the audience you are trying to reach.

Also watch out for the smaller agency that may not have the talent, research, or other capabilities needed by larger firms and by most companies involved with consumer products. In these cases, it may be better to opt for your own in-house operation rather than the "too small" agency.

Pearl #5: Be Sure You Are In Command

As the old Army officer's training manual had it, ". . . Give a command . . . make sure it is understood, and walk away fully expecting it will be carried out." This is also the best policy to adopt with either your ad agency or staff. Do not try to second guess or arbitrarily countermand your own orders. Listen carefully to recommendations and, once a direction has been agreed upon, let the agency or your people do the job without interference or additional suggestions. There are no more frustrated people in the world than professional copywriters and artists who are constantly being undermined with afterthoughts from the manager after the direction of a program has been established and creative ideas are being set in motion.

You stay in charge by leaving the agency or staff alone after you outline the assignment and its goals. In the case of the outside ad agency, once it puts it all together and presents its initial approach (rough art, copy platform, etc.), you may wish to add some final refinements. Or, if the agency is totally off target, then explain your objectives again along with your specific reasons for rejecting their ideas. If they return a second time with off-the-wall concepts that you are sure will not work, then fire them.

RESPONSIBILITY AND AUTHORITY

It is most important that management gives you full and final authority over the ad agency. If your agency's account representative feels he or she can go over your head for decisions, you are in the untenable position of having responsibility without authority and it might be well for you to start looking for another job.

You should, by all means, include all appropriate management people in the selection of the agency. However, make it very clear that you must have the *full authority* to fire the agency when you feel it is no longer serving your needs.

In this same regard, you should never attempt to lay blame on the agency. As far as management is concerned, the buck stops with you and, if the agency is not performing the way you wish, don't complain. Again, our suggestion is that you fire them quickly and avoid lingering pain and suffering on both sides.

Pearl #6: No Secrets . . . No Surprises

Be honest and candid with the agency (or with your staff if you set up an in-house operation). Do not play it close to the vest and, above all, keep everyone updated on any changes in your overall plan, corporate goals, strategies, and budgets. This is the only way the agency can produce programs that keep up with your needs and objectives. Your account team or staff can help only as far as they are informed of any and all changes. Remember, your job as a manager of communications is to understand your company—its products and its policies. You must be willing and able to communicate these in order to obtain meaningful and effective promotions.

Pearl #7: Manage Is the Name of Your Job . . . Do It, Don't Duck It

Here is where we come to a difficult turn. Throughout this book, we have tried to provide specific, practical, "how-to" information on doing your job as communicator. Now, we must remind you that simply because you know how to do it does not mean that you, yourself, have to do it. We feel that it is most important to keep the functions of communications manager and creative director separate. They, of course, must overlap and your creative talent will come into play as you direct the efforts of your staff, if you have an in-house operation, or your agency, if that is the direction you have chosen. It has been our experience that there is a great temptation for new managers to become overinvolved with the day-to-day details, at the expense of directing the overall operation. Your staff or agency knows how to do a specific job; you, as manager, must be more concerned about *why* they are doing that specific job. So, find the agency or develop a staff with creative power and the expertise to handle detail and rely on that team completely. It is important to remember that the ability to recognize talent is a talent itself. Be prepared to defend your agency or staff as if their work were your own because your direction and approval indeed makes it so.

In this same regard, be careful that upper management does not get too far into your act. Overdirection from the top is the main reason why an in-house agency—and its managers—fail.

Too often, we have seen a marketing vice president or even a chief executive of a company become a stumbling block by placing unreasonable constraints and reductions on an already-established budget. The greatest threat of all is management who makes part of your task that of saving money. If you cannot convince those in charge that the promotional budget is an investment and not an expense, you had better start polishing up the old resume.

Pearl #8: Take a Chance. . . Life Is an Adventure or It Is Nothing at All

The smaller the available budget, the greater the need for exceptional creative efforts. Phrased another way, good creative talent often can make up for what is sometimes lacking in dollars. However, this often means *taking a risk*. We have all seen low-budget programs outdo expensive campaigns because of new, dynamic approaches smartly executed. Sensational promotions are not a fluke. They are produced by creative people who know the product and how to sell it, *and* creative and courageous communications managers who know when to take a chance.

Pearl #9: Be a Pro . . . Don't Get Sloppy

Whatever you do, do it to the best of your ability. Professionals do not allow spelling and grammar errors to slip by. Nor do they let slipshod work of any kind pass as a final effort. Everyone makes a mistake now and again and errors are bound to occur, but the price of professionalism is eternal vigilance. It is up to you to check and recheck everything that leaves your office. Remember, there is never enough time to do it right but there is always enough time to do it over.

One of the most disappointing and frustrating experiences in life is to do a job incredibly fast, because there was no time, and cut costs to the bone, because there was no money, and wind up with a promotional piece that did not work (the most expensive kind of all). We have seen brochures that were put together under extremely tight deadlines, very limited budgets, and after a while no one remembered any of that. All that remained was a work that reflected an amateur company, with amateur products, produced by an amateur group, directed by an amateur manager. No one will even ask why it turned out so bad, only why it was left to amateurs.

Pearl #10: The Communications Manager . . . The "All Seasons" Person

In order to be an effective and successful communications manager, you will be called on to play many roles. You will also have to be:

- A psychologist—to understand how best to motivate the prospects and customers to buy

- A diplomat—to deal with top management who sometimes feel that their instincts are better than tried-and-true methods derived from a business plan

- A super-salesperson—to sell good ideas and a reasonable budget to management

- A communicator—to be persuasive and effective, both verbally and with the written word

- A decision maker—to have a special feeling for new concepts and ideas and to be unafraid to take some risks

and most importantly

- An attentive human being who has the special ability to listen carefully in order to act wisely.

Writing ads, checking proofs, setting up photo sessions, evaluating publications, running trade shows, getting out publicity releases, putting together promotional plans, making schedules and budgets, selecting printers and other suppliers, putting together direct mail programs, critiquing radio and TV commercials, changing light bulbs, and directing the entire shooting match—if you can do all this and much, much more, and not count the cost, then you indeed have become a professional communicator.

Index

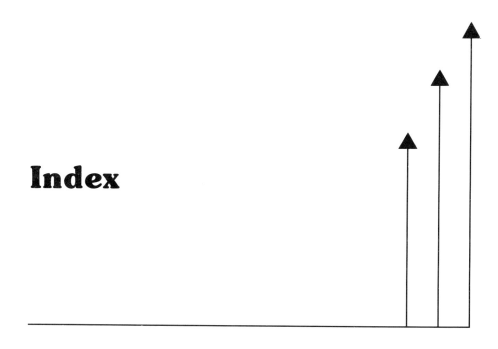